Complete Guide to the
Broads
Bridget Lely

G000280769

Welcome to the Broads

Ever since adventurous Victorians discovered the appeal of sailing through this enchanted land of lazy waterways, the Broads have been a favourite holiday destination for many thousands of people. There are few places where it is quite so satisfying to be messing about in or near boats.

The rivers and broads provide opportunities for boating, fishing, birdwatching, walking and just enjoying the peace and tranquillity of getting back to nature. Nearby villages and bustling market towns have their own attractions, and there's nothing quite like a pint of local ale at a riverside pub.

Feeding ducks at How Hill

But there is plenty more to discover in this diverse region, from the medieval streets, castle and cathedral of the city of Norwich, with its buzzing nightlife, to the peaceful dunes of the eastern coastline and the varied pleasures of such seaside resorts as Great Yarmouth and Lowestoft.

A rare environment

The meandering network of rivers and broads and surrounding low-lying countryside forms one of Britain's national parks, protected and cared for by the Broads Authority. The area is a haven for wildlife, with species like the swallowtail butterfly and the Norfolk brown hawker dragonfly, found nowhere else in the country, and in spring the boom of the bittern can sometimes be heard among the reedbeds.

The broads themselves, sixty or so shallow lakes, are linked by five rivers – the Bure, Yare, Ant, Thurne and Waveney – which flow through wooded countryside and grazing marshes, passing picturesque mills or windpumps.

Fun afloat

With 125 miles *[200 km]* of lock-free navigable waterways, the best way of exploring is, of course, by boat, whether on board a cruiser or dayboat, wherry, yacht or canoe. Boatyards throughout the river system offer craft for hire, and launching facilities and private moorings are available for boat owners.

Larger riverboats take local tours, the graceful sailing wherries also carry passengers and water trails at nature reserves provide the opportunity to discover the wildlife of the rivers and dykes in quiet electric- or solar-powered passenger boats.

Relaxing at Stalham

Water sports are well catered for, with opportunities to learn or improve your skills at sailing, canoeing and windsurfing at several local centres.

Bankside angling is good throughout the area, and dinghies can be hired from the boatyards.

... and on land

The rivers and most of the broads can be reached by road, as can a number of restored windpumps – and riverside pubs, cafés and restaurants provide many pleasant stopping places. The quiet lanes through gently rolling countryside make cycling and walking a pleasure. Local nature reserves have walking trails and secluded bird hides.

Historic houses, country gardens and parks, ruined castles and abbeys, craft workshops and animal parks are all within

Oby Mill, River Bure

reach, as are a variety of sporting and other leisure facilities. Local rail and bus services help river-based visitors to explore towns and villages beyond the waterways.

Access for all

Organisations and businesses are working towards improving accessibility in the Broads, to help as many people as possible experience its special magic. There is an increasing range of opportunities for getting on the water, with wheelchair-accessible trip and day hire boats, fishing dinghies and the opportunity to learn to sail (see page 41). Some places also have facilities for people with visual or hearing impairments.

Bittern

Botaurus stellaris

This rare and elusive bird hides in dense reedbeds, pointing its beak to the sky and stretching its long neck when disturbed, to blend with the reeds. It feeds on fish, eels, frogs and small mammals. The distinctive low booming call of the male can be heard in spring and summer at local reserves.

Welcome to the Broads

Beccles, a charming market town

There are wheelchair-accessible boardwalks through the mysterious and swampy 'carr' woodlands at Barton, Filby, Cockshoot, Hickling, Ranworth and Wheatfen, and fishing platforms near Cockshoot and at Rollesby Bridge.

The ***Broads Information Centres*** (see page 8) have more details of local facilities. Information centres at Beccles, Hoveton and Ranworth are wheelchair accessible, and all centres have induction loops.

Places to stay

The Broads has a wide choice of campsites, self-catering accommodation, B & Bs, guesthouses and hotels, providing places to stay throughout the area, in town or village, farmhouse or cottage, by a river or near the coast. Local information centres can help with booking, and many places have their own websites. The Broads Authority annual magazine, *broadcaster*, is full of information. Booking agencies and many boatyards also offer holiday homes.

Roots

The Complete Guide to the Broads has its roots in *What to Do on the Norfolk Broads*, a much loved annual publication. During the mid-1930s an Anglo-American named Drew Miller, who lived in Dydler's Mill near Horning, travelled the waterways, making meticulous notes. He produced the first edition of *What to Do on the Norfolk Broads* in 1935, in friendly competition with Claud Hamilton, the author of *Hamilton's Navigations*.

In more recent years the book, published by Jarrold and updated annually, contained tide tables, advertisements of local businesses and detailed listings of facilities in every waterside village. Copies of early editions of *What to Do on the Norfolk Broads* are much sought after by collectors.

This book continues the tradition of following the routes of the many waterways in the *Rivers and broads* section and seeks to give general information about facilities and interesting attractions within easy reach of the rivers – invaluable to all those who want to explore this fascinating region by land or water.

Enjoying local ale at the Fur and Feather, Woodbastwick

Electric Eel on the water trail at How Hill

The origins of the broads themselves go back to the need for slow-burning fuel for heating and cooking in medieval times. Peat pits were dug in boggy areas of Norfolk between the ninth and fourteenth centuries, and these diggings gradually became flooded as water levels rose, forming shallow, broad areas of water.

A working wherry

The broads are connected by rivers, and for centuries these waterways were an important route for transporting goods between local villages and towns. Each village has a quay, or staithe, where cargo could be unloaded. Single-sailed trading boats, known as wherries, were used to carry agricultural products including corn, reeds and sedge, as well as timber, coal and even cement.

Norfolk reed

Phragmites australisis

The stalks of wild reed are cut between Christmas and April for use by thatchers, after frosts and winds have removed the leaves. A scythe or sickle is used to cut the hard fibrous stems. The reed is carried in bundles tied with a sedge or willow band on flat-bottomed boats known as 'lighters'.

Introduction to the Broads

The Broads were discovered as a holiday destination over a hundred years ago. John Loynes, who started by hiring his own boat to friends, designed a selection of cruising boats and set up a boatyard at Wroxham Bridge in 1880. By the early twentieth century the development of the railway had helped to make Broads holidays possible for a growing number of visitors, and over 40 owners were offering boats for hire.

The Broads continued to grow in popularity, and were probably at their height during the 1970s. Nowadays many who come to enjoy the peaceful atmosphere are based on land, but boatyards continue to offer opportunities for short or long breaks on comfortable modern cruisers as well as more traditional craft.

The Norfolk wherry

Early freight vessels, known as keels, were single-masted and square-rigged. The first wherries were actually light rowing craft for passengers, with four oarsmen. A new rigging system that was introduced from Holland in the sixteenth century, with the sail fore-and-aft, meant that river craft could sail close to the wind and make better progress against headwinds, and this proved ideal for the easily manoeuvred wherries.

Wherries grew in size over the centuries and could eventually carry up to 40 tons of cargo. They were clinker built from oak, with a counter-balanced mast that was easily lowered to pass under bridges. The hold stretched back from the mast, and a tiny cabin had two bunks and a stove for the crew. Some wherries were steered by tiller – others had a cockpit with room for one steersman. The boats ceased trading in 1950, but some were converted or commissioned as holiday craft, and there are still seven wherries afloat.

Wherries Hathor *and* Olive *on Wroxham Broad*

Reedbeds

Beside the rivers and broads there are often wide beds of reeds. In the past these provided the raw materials for thatching, and some continue to be the source of reed and sedge for modern-day thatchers. A thatched roof is cool in summer and cosy in winter, and will last for between 50 and 70 years, so there is still a steady demand for thatch on traditional cottages as well as modern buildings.

Reedbeds are an important habitat for wildlife, and sedgebeds also support other plants, including milk parsley, the food of the swallowtail butterfly. If beds are not managed by the traditional method of cutting, other plants and eventually trees will take hold, forming wet or 'carr' woodland.

A local thatcher at work

Beccles Marshes

Cutting reeds for thatching

Marshland

An intricate network of dykes was used to drain the low-lying marshland beside the rivers for farming use, and during the eighteenth century wind-powered drainage mills were built to help control the water levels. By the early nineteenth century over a hundred mills were in use, pumping water along the dykes and up into the embanked rivers. Technological improvements led to the use of steam pumps, and internal combustion engines were followed by the electric pumps in use today.

The marshes are grazed by cattle, sheep and horses, and the dykes provide the home for a thriving wildlife, including dragonflies and damselflies. Farmers receive subsidies to keep the fields for their traditional grazing use.

The Broads National Park

The Broads Authority is responsible for conservation, recreation and navigation. It keeps the waterways open and safe and provides free moorings. Navigation rangers, who patrol the rivers, are available for

Sedge

Cladium mariscus

Sedge is harvested from beds beside the rivers and broads between June and October. It is used on the ridges of thatched roofs, as it is more flexible than reed.

Introduction to the Broads

advice and help, and also enforce speed limits – imposed for safety and to limit bank erosion. All boats pay a toll towards the upkeep of the waterways.

The Broads Authority is the planning authority, as well as working to restore and enhance the natural wildlife habitats of the area. It also helps private owners and wildlife organisations to manage the reedbeds, with the support of hard-working conservation volunteers.

Other Broads Authority conservation projects include working with the Environment Agency to restore clear water to the rivers and broads so that wildlife can flourish.

Coot on Barton Broad

Broads Information Centres provide expert help with all the practical details of a holiday in the area.

Green boating

It's now possible to use environmentally friendly craft on the waterways, either by hiring an electrically powered dayboat, or taking a trip on one of several Broads Authority boats: the solar-powered *Ra* on Barton Broad, the *Electric Eel* at How Hill, or *Helen*, a Broads reed lighter at Ranworth. The elegant *Liana*, based at Beccles, offers a taste of Edwardian style on trips along the River Waveney.

Visiting boat users can help to protect the rivers by using biodegradable products for washing up, taking care not to spill diesel fuel or oil, and using the special sites for rubbish. Avoiding noise pollution means that everyone can enjoy the special peace of the waterways.

Electric power charging points can be found at Coltishall, Hickling, Horning, Ludham Bridge, Potter Heigham, Norwich, Stalham and Wroxham. Payment is made by cards obtained from Broads Information Centres.

Broadland villages and towns

Many of the charming villages still have a shop or two, a picturesque medieval church and at least one tempting riverside pub. There are also small boatyards throughout the area, with friendly staff who are happy to help.

Local towns have a good selection of shops and places to eat, and several have information offices to help visitors discover more. In some towns regular markets offer a wide variety of goods – a few, such as Stalham and Beccles, now also hold farmers' markets, where local food can be bought direct from the producer.

Many visitors start their Broads holiday at Wroxham and Hoveton, together known as the 'capital' of the Broads. This is also an excellent shopping centre.

Broads Information Centres

Centres open daily Easter/April–October

Beccles, The Quay, Fen Lane.
Tel: 01502 713196

Hoveton/Wroxham, Station Road.
Tel: 01603 782281

How Hill, Ludham. Toad Hole Cottage Museum and *Electric Eel* Wildlife Water Trail.
Tel: 01692 678763

Potter Heigham, Bridge Road.
Tel: 01692 670779

Ranworth, The Staithe.
Tel: 01603 270453

Whitlingham Visitor Centre,
Whitlingham Lane, Trowse, Norwich
Tel: 01603 617332

Winter enquiries: Broads Authority,
18 Colegate, Norwich NR3 1BQ
Tel: 01603 610734
www.broads-authority.gov.uk

Nature reserves

Wildlife is a vital part of the character of the Broads and the area has many peaceful nature reserves, some of national and international importance. The public are welcome to visit them. Most have nature trails with information boards and some have visitors' centres. Boardwalks help to make reserves more accessible, but paths are often muddy, so boots are useful. Binoculars make it easier to identify the wildlife.

Broads area

Alderfen Broad (NWT) 2 miles *[3.2 km]* N of Horning off A1062. Varied wildfowl, dragonflies and damselflies.

Settlement lagoons for mud at Barton Broad

Barton Broad (NWT) 1 mile *[1.6 km]* S of Stalham off A1151, near Neatishead. Part of a National Nature Reserve. A dying broad in the mid 1990s, clogged with algae, revitalised by pumping nutrient-rich mud into nearby lagoons. A boardwalk at Herons' Carr leads through carr woodland to a platform, with panoramic views of the broad. Trips on *Ra* from Gay's Staithe, 1 mile [1.6 km] from Neatishead on the Irstead road. Tel: 01603 782281

Berney Marshes (RSPB) W of Great Yarmouth. Part of the Halvergate grazing marshes, where wading birds such as lapwing, redshank and snipe breed. In winter large flocks of wildfowl visit the reserve. Access by boat (moorings at Berney Arms) or by public footpath. The Norwich-Great Yarmouth train stops at Berney Arms Halt.

Breydon Water (RSPB) Next to Great Yarmouth, close to the estuary of the River Yare. At low tide, mudflats are exposed on either side of a wide deep channel dredged for shipping. Home to waders and wildfowl, with footpaths along the shores and a bird hide at the eastern end.

Exploring Ranworth Broad aboard Helen

Broads Wildlife Centre (NWT), Ranworth. 1 mile *[1.6 km]* N of South Walsham off B1140. A ¼-mile *[400 m]* nature trail from the village leads visitors on a boarded walkway through a typical Broads environment to the floating conservation centre. Exhibition on conservation and wildlife, and birdwatching gallery. Tel: 01603 625540. Guided boat trips from staithe, booking essential. Tel: 01603 270453

Plant cages at Ranworth Broad

Carlton Marshes (SWT) At end of Burnt Hill Lane, Carlton Colville off A146. Flowering aquatic plants, wading birds and birds of prey, dragonflies and glow-worms in summer. Dogs on leads only. Visitor centre. Tel: 01502 564250

Cockshoot Broad (NWT) 1 mile *[1.6 km]* downstream of Horning. Access via boardwalk from moorings at Cockshoot Dyke, or from riverside car park at Woodbastwick, off B1140. Isolated from the River Bure, the broad has had nutrient-rich mud pumped out. The resulting clear water has allowed a recovery of the wildlife. Birdwatching hide.

Foxburrow Wood (SWT) Access from Gunton Church Lane, Lowestoft, off A12. Bluebells in spring and other flowers typical of ancient woodland. Ponds, ditches and streams, and birds including nuthatch, woodpecker and treecreeper. Summer visitors include blackcap, chiffchaff and willow warbler.

Grey heron

Ardea cinerea

The heron, with its grey and white plumage, is a familiar sight throughout the Broads, often standing stock-still on one leg, waiting for a catch. Their food includes fish, frogs, eels and insects, and sometimes young waterfowl. The large nests are made of branches and sticks, usually high in a tree. Herons are easy to identify in flight, with their wide dark-tipped grey wings flapping elegantly.

Nature reserves

Hickling Broad National Nature Reserve (NWT) 2 miles *[3.25 km]* N of Potter Heigham off A149. Open reed- and sedge-beds and oak woodland, with passage waders in spring and autumn, bittern, heron, bearded tit, dragonflies and swallowtail butterfly in summer. Access via Stubb Road. Visitor centre. Nature trails and 2-hour water trail in a traditional reed lighter – advance booking essential. Tel: 01692 598276.

Horsey Mere (NT) Access to Horsey Mere by boat only from the River Thurne, Hickling Broad or from Horsey Staithe alongside B1159 3 miles *[4.75 km]* NW of Winterton. Winter wildfowl and birds of passage. Shop and toilets. Footpath to viewpoint over broad and to beach.

Hoveton Great Broad (EN) 2 miles *[3.25 km]* SE of Wroxham, upstream from Salhouse Broad. Only accessible by boat, with nature trail through fen and woodland to the broad. Tel: 01603 598400

Waterlilies, a sign of clear water

How Hill (Broads Authority) 1½ miles *[2.5 km]* N of Ludham Bridge off A1062. Wildlife walking trail past windpumps and through fens and woodlands. Toad Hole Cottage Museum, an eel-catcher's cottage, housing Broads Information Centre. Wildlife water trail on the *Electric Eel*. Book in advance. Tel: 01692 678763

Martham Broad National Nature Reserve (NWT) 1¼ miles *[2 km]* NE of Martham. Open water, reed and sedge fen with swallowtail butterflies in June and July.

Oulton Marshes (SWT) Access from Church Lane, Oulton. Meadows with many rare plants, breeding birds, including grasshopper, reed and sedge warblers and Cetti's warbler, dragonflies and damselflies. Dogs on leads only.

Strumpshaw Fen

Strumpshaw Fen National Nature Reserve (RSPB) 7 miles *[11.25 km]* E of Norwich off A47. Broads, reedbeds and woodland, with a variety of birds, including kingfishers, marsh harriers and overwintering migrants. Meadowland with wildflowers, butterflies and dragonflies. Hides, including an information hide. Tel: 01603 715191

Surlingham Church Marsh (RSPB) 5 miles *[8 km]* E of Norwich off A146. Former grazing marsh with dykes and pools. Nesting marsh harriers, warblers and other summer migrants. Circular walk of 1½ miles *[2.5 km]* from Surlingham church. Tel: 01603 715191

Upton Fen (NWT), 4½ miles *[7 km]* from Acle off B1140 to South Walsham. Waymarked trails through open fen with pools and woodland. Particularly noted for dragonflies.

Wheatfen, Ted Ellis Nature Reserve, near Surlingham. Open fen, reedbeds, tidal channels, two broads and woodland, with 3-mile *[4.8 km]* nature trail. Tel: 01508 538036

The Norfolk coast

Norfolk is bounded by the sea in the north and east and has a number of interesting coastal reserves. The following are nearest to the Broads area.

Blakeney Point National Nature Reserve (NT/EN) 8 miles *[12.75 km]* W of Sheringham off A149. One of the largest expanses of undeveloped coastal habitat in Europe, with intertidal sands and muds, saltmarshes, shingle banks and sand-dunes, breeding colonies of several species of birds and a colony of seals. Access by boat from Blakeney or Morston. Hides and nature trails.

On the wildlife walking trail at How Hill

Cley Marshes (NWT) 6 miles *[9.5 km]* W of Sheringham. Wide expanse of reedbed, lagoons and grazing marsh, and home to a large number of rare migrants. Access by permit from visitor centre. Tickets from Watcher's Cottage. Tel: 01263 740008

Winterton Dunes National Nature Reserve (EN) 7 miles *[11.25 km]* N of Great Yarmouth. Wide area of sand-dunes with coastal birds and plants.

Conservation societies

Natural England
Tel: 0845 600 3078
www.naturalengland.org.uk

National Trust (NT)
Tel: 0870 458 4000
www.nationaltrust.org.uk

Norfolk Wildlife Trust (NWT)
Tel: 01603 625540
www.wildlifetrust.org.uk/norfolk

Royal Society for the Protection of Birds (RSPB) Tel: 01603 661662
www.rspb.org.uk

Suffolk Wildlife Trust (SWT)
Tel: 01473 890089
www.wildlifetrust.org.uk/suffolk

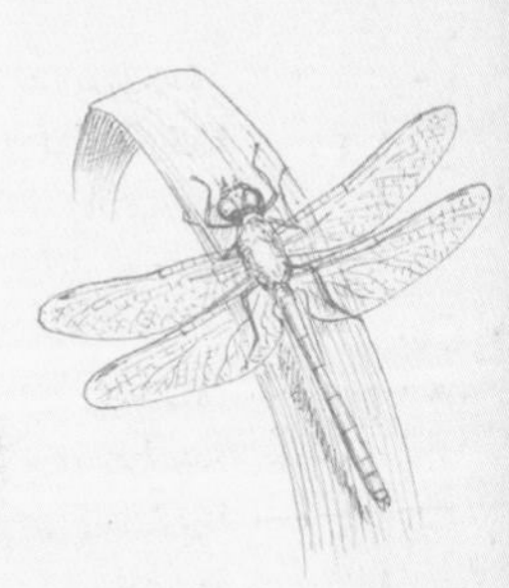

Norfolk hawker

Anaciaeschna isosceles

This rare dragonfly is only found in Norfolk and Suffolk and is the symbol of the Broads Authority. It has clear wings, large green eyes and its body is mid-brown with a yellow triangular mark on the second abdominal section. Adults fly from late May to mid-August, and rest on bushes and trees near clear water, which usually contains water soldier plants.

Wildlife

The environment of the Broads is carefully managed, preserving many sites of special interest to naturalists. A unique area, it is rich in wildlife – with some creatures easier to identify than others. These water birds are some of the most common.

Mallard drake

Mallard *Anas platyrhyncha*

The females are a mottled brown, but in spring the drakes develop a dark bottle-green head and reddish chest, with a brown back, grey sides and a white belly. Mallards dip down to feed, so that their tails pop up, and eat all kinds of small creatures and plants. They nest on the ground at the water's edge.

Great crested grebe

Great crested grebe

Podiceps cristatus

This is easily recognised from the tufts of its grey crest. Its back is grey, the sides chestnut-coloured and the breast and belly are white. In spring there is a black frill at the bottom of the neck. Grebes are graceful divers, feeding on fish, insects and shellfish. They nest among reeds, near the edge of open water.

Moorhens' nest

Moorhen *Gallinula chloropus*

Moorhens are small and almost black, with a white line along the side and a white patch under the tail. Their beaks are red, with yellow near the tip, and their heads jerk back and forth as they swim. They eat insects, worms, berries and seeds, and water animals and plants. Moorhens nest on the ground or in a bush or tree.

Coot with chick

Coot *Fulica atra*

Coots are like a larger version of a moorhen, but have a white patch on the front of the head and a white beak. Their feathers are black and their feet have webbing. They feed on water plants, worms, grain and shellfish, and nest amongst the reeds.

Greylag goose

Greylag goose *Anser anser*

Flocks of these geese are a common sight on the rivers and broads. Their plumage is light grey-brown with a white rump and they have stout pinkish-orange bills. They eat grain, as well as grass and other vegetation, and build large down-filled nests amongst the reeds.

Other Broadland birds

The skies, waterways, marshes and mudflats of the Broads also have a wide variety of less common birds. Many are local residents, but areas like Breydon Water are visited by large flocks of wintering waterfowl. These are a few of the other species that can be seen.

Bearded tit

Bearded tit *Panurus biarmicus*

Bearded tits, found in the area around Hickling, are known to local people as reed pheasants. The male is colourful, with a light bluish grey head, reddish body and black markings on either side of its bill, and its wings are striped with red and grey. The female is tawny coloured.

Lapwing

Lapwing *Vanellus vanellus*

The lapwing has a long dark upswept crest and distinctive dark glossy back and wings, with white sides to its head and a white belly. Lapwings breed on Berney Marshes, making their nests in slight dips in the ground. They eat a variety of insects.

Reed warbler

Reed warbler *acrocephalus scirpaceus*

This summer visitor sings from inside the reedbeds, so is not often seen. The song is a repetitive flow of short notes, but it also frequently imitates other birds. It feeds on insects and berries. The nest is a deep cup made of grass and moss, and usually suspended between reed stems.

Sedge warbler

Sedge warbler *Acrocephalus schoenobaenus*

A summer visitor from Africa, this small brown bird has a distinctive creamy stripe over the eye. Sedge warblers are far from secretive, uttering a loud and varied scolding song.

Male wigeon

Wigeon *Anas penelope*

Wigeon arrive from the Baltic in late summer, travelling east again for breeding in April. The males have a chestnut head, grey body and black and white rear. The females are plainer, with a brown back and pale underparts, but have the same characteristic shape. They congregate in winter around estuaries, feeding in shallow water or on grassland.

Short-eared owl

Asio flammeus

This owl lives in open fields, marshes and meadows, nesting in a scrape on the ground amongst reeds and grasses. Its back and wings are mottled pale buff and dark brown and the underparts are pale buff. The short 'ear tufts' are not easy to see. Hunting by day, it flies low, zig-zagging in search of field mice and other small rodents.

Wildlife

Fish

The broads and their linking tidal rivers provide varied conditions for fish. The upper reaches are slow flowing and narrow, but river currents are fast nearer the sea and there are surges of salt water. The broads are often still and in some places relatively deep.

Angling is good throughout the area. The coarse fishing season runs from 16 June to 14 March and Environment Agency licences are available from post offices. Fishing tackle can be bought in larger villages and machines supply bait in riverside locations.

Chub *Leuciscus cephalus*

The chub has large dark-edged scales. The dorsal fin and tail are greyish-green and the lower fins orange-red. It prefers shallow waters with a hard bed and feeds on insects, small fish, frogs and small fruit.

Roach *Rutilus rutilus*

A member of the carp family, the roach has a dark back with a blue or green sheen, silver-white sides and relatively large scales. The grey dorsal fin is above the pelvic fins. The other fins, apart from the tail, are reddish in colour. Roach feed on invertebrates and weed.

Bream *Abramis brama*

The bream has a high flattened body with lead-blue back and silver or sometimes golden sides. Its fins are dark grey and it has small eyes. Its protrusible mouth allows it to feed from the riverbed.

Perch *Perca fluviatilis*

The perch has a flat-sided body and two dorsal fins, the first quite spiny. The top of the fish is dark grey or blue to olive green with dark stripes around the sides and a light belly. The lower fins are red. Perch feed on invertebrates and small fish.

Tench *Tinca tinca*

Tench have small scales, firmly rooted in the skin. The back is brownish-green, the sides are golden and the belly is yellow. The eyes are small and there is a small barbel at each corner of the mouth. Tench feed on small invertebrates.

Fishing etiquette • Never fish from a moving boat • Give way to mooring boats • Never discard fishing tackle • Take litter home

Dragonflies and damselflies

Dykes and broads are safe breeding places for dragonflies and damselflies, providing clean water, water plants on which to lay eggs and space to hunt for small insects. Reeds and bushes supply shelter.

Damselflies are small, with four equal wings, and stay close to water because their flight is weak. They rest with wings folded along the length of their body. Their eyes are clearly separated and never touching. Dragonflies are larger, with hind wings that are shorter and broader than the forewings. The largest can fly at 10 mph and travel long distances, preying on flying insects. They rest with wings outstretched and their large closely set eyes usually touch.

Red-eyed damselfly *Erythromma najas*

The eyes of this common damselfly are distinctive. The male is greenish-blue with a clear band of blue at the tip of the abdomen and the wings are transparent. The female has no band on the abdomen and her eyes are duller. Males often sit on floating weeds and water lilies. They are in flight between mid-May and August.

Southern hawker

Aeschna cyanea

This large dragonfly has transparent wings. The body of the male has mottled patches of greens, yellows and blues with a large yellowy-green triangle on the second abdominal segment. There is no blue on the female. They are common between July and early October.

Butterflies

Many species of butterflies can be seen in the Broads, including several that are rare. Upton has white admirals, Strumpshaw swallowtails and holly blues, and swallowtails and purple hairstreaks can be seen at Hickling.

Purple hairstreak

Quercusia quercus

This common small butterfly lives in the canopies of oak trees. Its wings glow a deep purple when they catch the light. The local colony in oaks at Hickling can be seen from the tree hide in late June and July.

Swallowtail

Papilio machaon

One of the most rare British butterflies, the swallowtail breeds solely on milk parsley, which grows amongst reeds and sedge. The adults can be seen flying over open fens on still days in May and June, stopping to feed on thistles and ragged robin.

White admiral

Limenitis camilla

White admirals have dark wings with a curving white band. Their eggs are laid on honeysuckle. They can be seen from mid-June to mid-August, often feeding on the nectar of bramble flowers. The flight pattern is a series of short beats followed by a long glide.

Great crested newt

Triturus cristatus

This is the largest newt found in Britain. Adults are dark-coloured with small white spots, and a yellow belly. Newts breathe air and spend much of the year on land, returning to water to breed at the end of the winter. They are most active at night, feeding on land and in water on worms and small water creatures.

Norwich

Norwich, the capital of Norfolk, is an ancient and gracious city that is best explored on foot, since many of the finest medieval buildings are hidden away down narrow alleys and streets, such as Elm Hill. (See map inside back cover.) The stone keep of Norwich Castle dates from the eleventh century, as does the imposing Norwich Cathedral, surrounded by the Close, a pleasantly peaceful area in which to wander.

The market place, which was moved to its present position in Norman times, is still the centre of the city, overlooked by the 1930s City Hall, with its high clock tower. The thirteenth-century flint-faced Guildhall was the seat of government in Norwich for five centuries. On the other side of the market is St Peter Mancroft, the most impressive of the thirty-one medieval churches in Norwich. Beyond that is the Forum, a modern addition to the city landscape, which, as well as housing the central library and hi-tech learning facilities, and the local BBC studios, has Origins, a multi-media exploration of the history of the region, as well as the Tourist Information Centre and a restaurant and café-bar.

Pull's Ferry, ancient access to Norwich Cathedral

Museums, galleries and other attractions

There are several museums, including Norwich Castle, in the city centre, and many small art galleries. The Sainsbury Centre for Visual Arts is on the outskirts at the University of East Anglia.

In summer there are regular themed walking tours with a Blue Badge guide, starting from the Tourist Information Centre at the Forum, and there are free guided walks around Norwich Cathedral several times a day. Open-top bus tours also run.

Bridewell Museum (NMS), Bridewell Alley. Focuses on Norwich life and industry. Tel: 01603 629127

City of Norwich Aviation Museum, Horsham St Faith. Includes a Vulcan bomber from the Falklands Task Force. Tel: 01603 893080 www.cnam.co.uk

Dragon Hall, King Street. Restored medieval merchant's trading hall near the river. Tel: 01603 592261 www.nhbg.fsnet.co.uk/dragon.htm

Inspire, St Michael's Church, Coslany Street. Provides hands-on experience of a variety of scientific exhibits. Accessible to all. Tel: 01603 612612 www.inspirediscoverycentre.com

Norwich Castle (NMS). The county's principal museum is packed with diverse treasures, including ancient gold jewellery, silver, porcelain and Roman pottery.

Norwich Castle

There are hands-on exhibits, models, video screens and computer animation. The gallery collection includes works by the Norwich School of painters and there are regular loans from Tate. Tel: 01603 493625

Origins, The Forum. A journey of exploration over the last 2000 years. Tel: 01603 727950 www.originsnorwich.co.uk

Plantation Garden, Earlham Road. Peaceful restored Victorian town garden in a chalk quarry. www.plantationgarden.co.uk

Royal Norfolk Regimental Museum (NMS), Market Avenue. Follows the story of Norfolk soldiers and their families. Tel: 01603 493650

The Forum and St Peter Mancroft Church

Sainsbury Centre for Visual Arts, University of East Anglia, Earlham Road. This award-winning building houses paintings and sculptures from around the world and hosts visiting exhibitions. Families are particularly welcome on the first Sunday of each month. Tel: 01603 593199 www.scva.org.uk

Strangers' Hall (NMS), Charing Cross. Displays of English domestic life. Public tours on Wed and Sat. For tickets, Tel: 01603 493636

USAAF 2nd Air Division Memorial Library, The Forum. Dedicated to nearly 7,000 young airmen stationed in Norfolk and North Suffolk who died in the Second World War. Tel: 01603 774747 www.2ndair.org.uk

Shopping

The city has a wide range of shops, from the intimate specialist supplier to national chain stores and supermarkets, and including three large department stores. There are a number of entrances to the Castle Mall, an imaginative shopping complex, which lies in an area excavated beside the Castle itself, and the Chapelfield Shopping Centre.

Pay spaces for parking can be found in the central streets, and there are large car parks within the centre, as well as a park and ride system from several sites on the outskirts of the city.

Cow Tower

An important part of the city's medieval defences, Cow Tower stands on the route of the Riverside Walk, which follows the banks of the River Wensum from Carrow Bridge through the historic industrial heart of the city to Hellesdon, 5 miles *[8 km]* upstream. The walk can be joined at many points, and also passes school playing fields beside the cathedral.

Museum services

Norfolk Museums Service (NMS)
museums.norfolk.gov.uk

Norwich

The Royal Arcade

Entertainment

Norwich offers a choice of professional and amateur theatres, a puppet theatre and outdoor performances through *Theatre in the Parks* during July and August. There are both mainstream multiplexes and an art-house cinema, and regular concerts are held in several venues.

The Norfolk and Norwich Festival and Open Studios events are held in May and the annual Beer Festival in the last week in October. The Lord Mayor's Celebrations take place on the weekend of the second Saturday in July.

There were once 365 pubs in the city – many now serve real ale and good food, and live music of varied styles can be found on most nights of the week. The numerous fine restaurants serve a wide range of food from around the world.

Nightlife is lively in Norwich throughout the year, particularly at the weekends, with a large number of clubs centred on the area around Prince of Wales Road.

Assembly House, Theatre Street. Concerts, art exhibitions. Tel: 01603 626402 www.assemblyhousenorwich.co.uk

Cinema City, St Andrew's Street. Art house and mainstream films. Tel: 01603 622047 www.cinemacity.co.uk

Hollywood Cinema, Anglia Square. Multiplex. Tel: 01603 621903 www.hollywoodcinemas.net

Maddermarket Theatre, St John's Alley. Professionally created productions staged by and for the community. Tel: 01603 620917 www.maddermarket. co.uk

Norwich Arts Centre, St Benedict's Street. Performing arts. Box office tel: 01603 660352 www.norwichartscentre.co.uk

Norwich Playhouse, St George's Street. Touring drama, dance, comedy and music. Tel: 01603 598598 www.norwichplayhouse.co.uk

Norwich Puppet Theatre, St James, Whitefriars. Seasons of imaginative productions. Tel: 01603 629921 www.puppettheatre.co.uk

The Riverside leisure complex

The Ribs of Beef riverside pub

MyVue, Castle Mall. Multiplex.
Tel: 08712 240240 www.myvue.com

St Andrew's and Blackfriars' Halls
Concert halls, sales and exhibitions.
Tel: 01603 628477 wwww.norwich.gov.uk

Theatre Royal, Theatre Street. One of the finest provincial theatres with leading productions. Tel: 01603 630000
www.theatreroyalnorwich.co.uk

Odeon Norwich, Wherry Road. Multiplex.
Tel: 0871 2244007 www.odeon.co.uk

Sports

Norwich is a very green city with several nature reserves, and large parks where a wide variety of outdoor sports take place. It is even possible to learn to ski on a dry slope. Water sports tuition is available and indoor sports, including swimming, are pursued at a number of local leisure centres. There are also a number of health and fitness centres.

There is a developing network of on- and off-road cycle routes, linking to the National Cycle Route 1 (Hull–Harwich) via part of Marriott's Way.

Broadland Aqua Park, Norwich Sport Village Hotel, Drayton High Road, Hellesdon. Swimming pools and indoor sports halls. Tel: 01603 788912

Norwich City Football Club,
Carrow Road. Tel: 01603 760760
www.canaries.co.uk

Norfolk County Cricket Club,
Manor Park Sports Ground, Horsford.
Tel: 01603 424635
www.norfolkccc.co.uk

Norfolk Ski Club, Whitlingham Lane, Trowse. Tel: 01603 662781
www.norfolkskiclub.com

Riverside Swimming Centre, Wherry Road. Pool, gym, crèche, sauna, steam room and spa. Tel: 01603 625166
www.leisureconnection.co.uk

Sportspark, University of East Anglia, Earlham Road. Swimming pool and a wide variety of other activities.
Tel: 01603 592398 www.sportspark.co.uk

Whitlingham Country Park,
Whitlingham Lane, Trowse. Water sports, pay as you play. Tel: 01603 632307
www.nycsoutdooreducation.co.uk

The River End terrace of Norwich City Football Club

Information centre

Tourist Information Centre,
The Forum. General information, National Express and national rail bookings. Open Apr–Oct
Mon–Sat 10.00–18.00, Sun 10.30–16.30; Nov–Mar Mon–Sat 10–17.30. Tel: 01603 727927
www.norwich.gov.uk

Red admiral

Vanessa atalanta

This butterfly has sooty black wings with scarlet bands and white spots. Red admirals are migrants that arrive in spring and breed in this country. The broods they produce can be seen during August and September.

Great Yarmouth

North Quay

Great Yarmouth is one of Britain's most popular seaside resorts, situated on the country's driest coastline and with a wide range of attractions for holidaymakers. The town is built on a spit of land between the sea and the River Yare and has four miles of broad sandy beach with two piers, a leisure centre, and innumerable other entertainments and activities along Marine Parade. There are firework displays on Saturday nights during the summer and a variety of other special events, including carnivals, band concerts and a maritime festival in September.

Great Yarmouth also has a proud maritime history. One of the most important harbours for the North Sea fishing fleet, the town was synonymous with herring fishing from before the twelfth century, and a severe food shortage in Norwich in 1666 was only averted by huge catches of herring brought ashore at Yarmouth.

In the first half of the twentieth century, the herring were gutted at high speed by Scottish fishergirls, who followed the fleet up and down the east coast, and a large proportion of the fish were smoked to produce bloaters and kippers in special smoke houses on the quayside. It was sometimes possible, during the autumn fishing season, to walk across the harbour from boat to boat. Drifters are no longer seen in the harbour, but herring are still brought into Yarmouth by the longshore fishermen.

Museums and historic attractions

Anna Sewell House, birthplace of the author of *Black Beauty*, now a restaurant.

Elizabethan House Museum (NT), South Quay. Home life through the ages. Tel: 01493 855746 www.nationaltrust.org.uk

Great Yarmouth Potteries and Old Fish Smoking Works, Trinity Place. Herring smoking museum, pottery workshops and nautical giftshop. Tel: 01493 850585

Museum Exhibition Galleries (NMS), Central Library, Tolhouse Street. Changing local and travelling exhibitions. Tel: 01493 844551 www.great-yarmouth.gov.uk

Norfolk Nelson Museum, South Quay. The life and times of Admiral Lord Nelson, England's greatest naval hero. Tel: 01493 850698. www.nelson-museum.co.uk

Nelson's Monument, Monument Road. Viewing from outside only.

Greyfriars' Cloisters, Row 117, South Quay (EH). Franciscan friary with early wall paintings. Open on Heritage Open Days. Tel: 01493 857900

Row 111 and Old Merchant's House, South Quay (EH). Tour of contrasting seventeenth-century town dwellings. Tel: 01493 857900 www.english-heritage.org.uk

St Nicholas' Church. Built in 1101, this is the largest parish church in England.

Time and Tide Museum, Blackfriars Road. A converted Victorian herring curing works detailing Great Yarmouth's fascinating maritime history. Tel: 01493 743930

Tolhouse Museum (NMS), Tolhouse Street. Early medieval building, once the courthouse and gaol, with original dungeons. Tel: 01493 858900

Stained glass at the Elizabethan House Museum

Tower Curing Works, Blackfriars Road. The story of Great Yarmouth from its beginnings to the present day.
Tel: 01493 745526

Town Hall, South Quay. Guided tours.
Tel: 01493 856100

Great Yarmouth Guided Heritage Walks – a choice of four walks. For further details, tel: 01493 846345 or 07901 915390

Shopping

Great Yarmouth has a good range of shopping facilities, including Market Gates Shopping Mall. The Market Place is one of the largest open-air markets in the country, with some stalls open six days a week. Recognised market days for the full market are Wednesdays and Saturdays, and Fridays during the summer.

Attractions

Amazonia, Marine Parade. Tropical jungle and gardens with reptiles from all over the world. Tel: 01493 842202

Britannia Pier, Marine Parade. Theatre, amusements, refreshments and licensed bars. Tel: 01493 842914

Docwras Rock Shop, Regent Road. Demonstrations of rock-making.
Tel: 01493 844676

House of Wax, Regent Road. Over 150 lifelike models of the famous.
Tel: 01493 844851

Joyland, Marine Parade.
Children's amusement and fun park.
Tel: 01493 844094

The Jungle, Marine Parade. Children's adventure play area at the Winter Gardens. Tel: 01493 845938

Merrivale Model Village, Marine Parade. Working models and fairground in landscaped gardens. Tel: 01493 842097
www.greatyarmouthmodelvillage.co.uk

North Drive Boating Lake.
Pedaloes, canoes and rowing boats for hire. Tel: 01493 844194

Observation Tower, Marine Parade. 120-foot *[36.5m]* observation tower on the seafront.

Pirates' Cove, Marine parade.
Golf adventure with putting course.
Tel: 01493 331785

The Log Flume ride at the Pleasure Beach

Pleasure Beach, South Beach Parade. Amusement park with rides and other attractions, gardens, licensed bar and refreshments. Tel: 01493 844585
www.pleasure-beach.co.uk

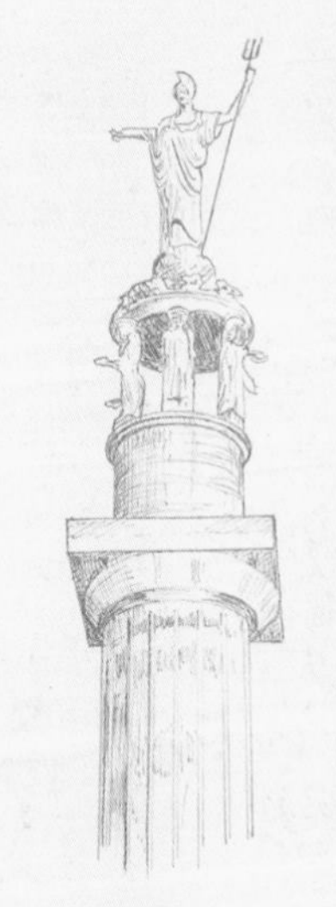

Nelson's Monument

Built in 1819, the monument to Norfolk-born Admiral Lord Nelson is 44 m *[144 ft]* high and has 217 stairs to a viewing platform (not open at present). The Norfolk Nelson Museum explores the story of this great naval hero.

Great Yarmouth

Sea cruises to view the seal colony on Scroby Sands from the beach on both the north and south sides of Britannia Pier, daily from May, depending on weather conditions.

Sealife Centre, Marine Parade. One of the country's biggest centres of underwater life, with 70 species of native sea creatures, restaurant and shop. Tel: 01493 330631 www.sealife.co.uk

Nightlife and live shows

Great Yarmouth has a number of lively clubs, pubs and bars, as well as casinos and theatre shows. The following venues present live shows.

Britannia Theatre, Marine Parade. Tel: 01493 842209

Hippodrome Circus, St George's Street. Tel: 01493 844172

Marina Centre, Marine Parade. Tel: 01493 851521

Pavilion Theatre, Pier Gardens, Gorleston. Tel: 01493 662832

St George's Theatre. King Street. Tel: 01493 858387

Winter Gardens, Marine Parade. Tel: 01493 843635

Cinema

Hollywood, Marine Parade. Multi-screen cinema. Tel: 01493 852600

Sports

Great Yarmouth has facilities for a wide range of sports, including angling, bowls, cricket, golf, go-karting, greyhound racing, horse racing, horse riding, putting, sailing, skateboarding, snooker, squash, stock-car racing, tennis and ten-pin bowling.

Marina Leisure and Fitness Centre, Marine Parade. Conference, exhibition, leisure and sports centre with swimming pool. Tel: 01493 851521

Phoenix Pool, Bradwell. Public swimming pool.

There is a putting green at Gorleston, as well as a model yacht pond and a paddling pool at Lower Parade.

Lifeboats and beach safety

The lifeboat station, on the riverside near the harbour mouth at Gorleston, is operated by the RNLI. The main lifeboat, RNLB *Samarbeta*, is supplemented by a three-man high-speed inflatable rescue craft. Shop open Sun–Fri. www.rnli.org.uk

Off-shore winds, use of inflatables dangerous and take extra care when bathing

Full-time beach guards patrol between Britannia and Wellington piers and at Gorleston, with boats and radios. Flags are used to warn of dangers.

First aid

The Jetty, Central Marine Parade. Tel: 01493 852812

Lower Promenade, Gorleston Tel: 01493 442876.

Accident and Emergency Department, James Paget Hospital, Lowestoft Road, Gorleston. Tel: 01493 452452

Information

Tourist Information Centre, Central Marine Parade. General information and accommodation booking service. Open Apr–Oct Mon–Sat 09.30–17.30; Sun 10.00–17.00. Tel: 01493 846345

Tourist Information Service, Town Hall. General information. Open all year weekdays 09.00–17.00. Tel: 01493 846345 www.great-yarmouth.co.uk

No swimming

Lowestoft

Suffolk's leading seaside resort, Lowestoft lies at the mouth of the River Waveney at the most easterly point in Britain. The older part of the town is built on cliffs, but south Lowestoft has award-winning sandy beaches. There are two fine piers and four and a half miles of promenade.

The town has a strong maritime history, with a harbour once filled with fishing fleets. A number of heritage vessels are moored in the harbour for all or part of the year. A Beach Village thrived during the eighteenth and nineteenth centuries, resulting in a series of narrow paths worn in the soft sloping cliff leading down from the High Street, still known as the Scores.

Lowestoft porcelain, produced during the eighteenth century, is much prized by collectors. Early examples were decorated with oriental-style blue designs under a pink-tinged glaze. A modern pottery is now producing hand-made porcelain here again, and the town has several antique dealers, art galleries and craft shops.

Among the many annual events, the spectacular Lowestoft Seafront Air Festival is not to be missed. Nearby Oulton Broad is one of the finest boating lakes in Britain and a popular centre for sailing, powerboat racing and fishing.

Powerboat racing on Oulton Broad

Museums

East Anglia Transport Museum, Carlton Colville. Working transport museum. Tel: 01502 518459 www.eatm.org.uk

Heritage (Workshop) Centre, High Street. Local heritage. Tel: 01502 587500

Lowestoft Maritime Museum, Sparrow's Nest Park, Whapload Road. History of the Lowestoft fishing fleets. Tel: 01502 561963

Lowestoft Museum, Nicholas Everitt Park, Oulton Broad. Lowestoft porcelain, local history and archaeology. Tel: 01502 511457

Royal Naval Patrol Service Association Museum, Sparrow's Nest. Tel: 01502 564344 www.rnps.lowestoft.org.uk

Entertainment

Free entertainment for children most Sunday afternoons and bank holidays at Sparrow's Nest Gardens

Claremont Pier, The Esplanade.

East Point Pavilion and Mayhem Adventure Play, Royal Plain. Tel: 01502 533600

Hollywood Cinema, London Road South. Tel: 01502 564567

Marina Theatre, The Marina. Tel: 01502 533200 www.marinatheatre.co.uk

Seagull Theatre, Pakefield. Tel: 01502 562863

Lowestoft porcelain

This soft paste porcelain was made in the town between 1756 and 1799. Early ware was decorated in pale tones of blue beneath a pink-tinged glaze. Later other colours were used over a glaze - the most typical being a dull khaki or deep green. In 1766 blue printed patterns were introduced. Many patterns and shapes are unique to Lowestoft ware.

Lowestoft

South Pier Leisure Complex, Royal Plain. Tel: 01502 512793

There are a number of nightclubs in the town. Check them out on: www.visit-lowestoft.co.uk

Beaches

Lowestoft beaches are clean and safe, with miles of gradually shelving golden sands. There are toilet and shower blocks, as well as many activities for children to enjoy, both outdoor and indoor, and lifeguard services on duty during the summer.

Any vessel using the waters within 150 metres *[164 yards]* of the mean low water mark must proceed with caution. The speed limit in the harbour is 4 knots.

Beach chalets for hire, Waveney District Council. Tel: 01502 523337

Beach officer. Tel: 01502 586167

Lifeguard station. Tel: 01502 523515

Excitement at New Pleasurewood Hills

Sports and outdoor activities

Bowls and tennis, plus other activities, at Nicholas Everitt Park at Oulton Broad, Kensington Gardens, Normanston Park and Sparrow's Nest. Putting greens at Denes Oval on Whapload Road, Kirkley Cliff on London Road South and Nicholas Everitt Park.

Bonds Meadow, Oulton Broad. Popular area for bird watching and walking dogs.

Caldecott Hall Golf and Leisure, Fritton. Tel: 01493 488488

Dip Farm Pitch and Putt, Corton Road. Tel: 01502 584348

East Point Family Golf, seafront next to East Point Pavilion.

New Pleasurewood Hills American Theme Park, Corton. 2 miles *[3.2 km]* N of Lowestoft off A12. Tel: 01502 586000 www.pleasurewoodhills.com

Pakefield Riding School, Carlton Rd. Tel: 01502 572257

Pets' Corner, Nicholas Everitt Park. Tel: 01502 563533

Pitch and Putt, next to the Thatched Roof Restaurant, Kirkley Cliff.

Rookery Park Golf Club Tel: 01502 509190

Waveney Sports and Leisure Centre, Water Lane. Swimming pool. Tel: 01502 569116

Water-based activities

Learn Scuba Diving Tel: 0845 2570131

Oulton Broad Water Sports Centre. Courses in windsurfing, sailing and canoeing. Tel: 01502 587163

Powerboat racing, Oulton Broad. Most Thurs and summer bank hols from 18.00. Tel: 01502 533600

Wayman Leisure RYA Windsurfing School and BCU Canoeing Tel: 01502 572014

Boat hire and trips

Excelsior Trust Tel: 01502 585302

Lowestoft Harbour Boat Tours Tel: 01502 569087

Myra Steam Yacht Classic Craft Chartering Tel: 01502 589014

Waveney River Tours, Mutford Lock, Bridge Road, Oulton Broad. Tel: 01502 574903

Information centre

East Point Pavilion Visitor Centre, Royal Plain. Open: Oct–Apr Mon–Fri 10.30–17.00, weekends and school holidays 10.00–17.00; Apr–end Sept daily 9.30–17.30. Closed Christmas Day, Boxing Day and New Year's Day. Tel: 01502 533600

Animal and wildlife collections

The Broads area offers opportunities to see otters, European wildfowl, muntjac deer or local sea creatures at close quarters, and to watch working horses demonstrate their skills. There are pets and farm animals to feed and handle, and the chance to encounter creatures from further afield at collections of reptiles and Asian and African wildlife.

A tiger at Thrigby Hall Wildlife Gardens

Africa Alive!, Kessingland. 2 miles *[3 km]* S of Great Yarmouth off A12. African safari adventure. Tel: 01502 740291 www.africa-alive.co.uk

Amazonia, Marine Parade, Great Yarmouth. Tropical reptile jungle. Tel: 01493 842202

Dinosaur Adventure Park, Weston Park, Lenwade. 9 miles *[14.5 km]* NW of Norwich off A1067. Dinosaur trail, adventure play area, secret animal garden. Tel: 01603 876310 www.dinosauradventure.co.uk

Norfolk Shire Horse Centre, West Runton. 2 miles *[3.25 km]* E of Sheringham off A149. Working demonstrations, cart rides, agricultural museum, trekking centre. Tel: 01263 837339 www.norfolk-shirehorse-centre.co.uk

Pets' Corner, Nicholas Everitt Park, Oulton Broad. Tel: 01502 563533

Pettitts Animal Adventure Park, Camp Hill, Reedham. 6 miles *[9.5 km]* S of Acle off B1140. Amusement rides, adventure golf, Falabella horses, miniature monkeys, wallabies and pets. Tel: 01493 700094 www.pettitsadventurepark.co.uk

Redwings Horse Sanctuary, Caldecott Hall, Fritton. 6 miles *[9.5 km]* SW of Great Yarmouth off A143. Rescued horses, ponies and donkeys. Tel: 01508 481000 www.redwings.org.uk

Sealife Centre, Marine Parade, Great Yarmouth. Tel: 01493 330631 www.sealife.co.uk

Thrigby Hall Wildlife Gardens, near Filby. 7 miles *[11.25 km]* NW of Great Yarmouth off A1064. Asian mammals, birds and reptiles. Tel: 01493 369477 www.thrigbyhall.co.uk

Craft workshops

Norfolk Open Studios, held in May and June each year, provides the opportunity to see artists at work (see page 32). The following centres also focus on local crafts.

Alby Crafts, Erpingham. 5 miles *[8 km]* S of Cromer on A140. Working crafts complex. Tel: 01263 761590 www.albycrafts.co.uk

The Candlemaker. Stokesby

The Candlemaker, Stokesby. 3 miles *[4.75 km]* E of Acle off A1064. Hand-crafted candles. Tel: 01493 750242

Willow Farm Flowers Dried Flower Centre, Cangate, Neatishead. 3 miles *[4.75 km]* N of Wroxham off A1151. Tel: 01603 783588

Wroxham Barns, Tunstead Road, Hoveton. 1½ miles *[2.5 km]* N of Wroxham off B1354. Local craftsmen at work, craft shops, traditional family funfair and junior farm. Tel: 01603 783911 www.wroxham-barns.co.uk

Avocet

Recurvirostra avosetta

This graceful wading bird is a summer visitor that breeds on Berney Marshes. White with black bands on its wings, a black crown and back of the neck, it has a thin black upturned bill and pale blue legs.

Historic buildings

Norfolk has highest concentration of medieval churches in the world. Of the 900 churches built in the prosperous days of the wool trade, over 650 are still in use. The Norfolk Churches Trust and the Churches Conservation Trust care for nearly 40 of the redundant churches, several of which are open to visitors. There are also magnificent country mansions in the Broads area that can be visited, as well as Roman, Norman and other medieval remains.

Hardley church, near Loddon

Blickling Hall (NT). 1½ miles *[2.5 km]* NW of Aylsham on B1354. Jacobean redbrick mansion with gardens and parkland. Tel: 01263 738030

Bungay Castle, Cross Street. Remains of Norman castle with visitor centre. Tel: 01986 896156 www.bungay-suffolk.co.uk

Burgh Castle (EH). 3 miles *[5 km]* SW of Great Yarmouth, beside River Waveney. Remains of third-century Roman fort.

Caister Roman Site (EH), Caister-on-Sea. On A1064, 3 miles *[5 km]* N of Great Yarmouth. Remains of Roman commercial port.

Felbrigg Hall (NT). 2 miles *[3.25 km]* S of Cromer off B1436 near Felbrigg village. Seventeenth-century mansion in parkland with walled garden. Grand tour paintings, guided tours. Tel: 01263 837444

St Benet's Abbey, Ludham. Ruins of Benedictine monastery and derelict windpump.

Antiphoner at Ranworth church

St Helen's Church, Ranworth. Fourteenth-century church with high tower and visitor centre. A medieval antiphoner or service book is on display. Guided tours.

St Olaves Priory, St Olaves. Remains of thirteenth-century Augustinian priory. Tel: 01493 488609

Sandringham House. 8 miles *[12.75 km]* NE of Kings Lynn. Country retreat of HM The Queen. Magnificent late nineteenth-century mansion. Gardens with nature trail, museum of motor cars and dolls. Closed last two weeks in July. Tel: 01553 612908 www.sandringhamestate.co.uk

Somerleyton Hall

Somerleyton Hall and Gardens, Somerleyton. Victorian mansion, gardens with maze and miniature railway. Tel: 01502 734901 www.somerleyton.co.uk

Wolterton Hall and Park, 5 miles *[8 km]* N of Aylsham off A140, near Erpingham. Historic park and eighteenth-century mansion. Hall tours on Fri, park open daily. Tel: 01263 584175 www.manningtongardens.co.uk

Gardens and country parks

Many communities open their gardens in summer under the National Gardens Scheme to help raise money for charity. Watch for local adverts and see the current *Yellow Book* for details. The following are a mixture of established and new gardens and parks that open regularly, but not all daily, so please check opening times.

Fairhaven Water and Woodland Garden, South Walsham

Fairhaven Water and Woodland Garden, South Walsham. 9 miles *[14.5 km]* E of Norwich off B1140. Wooded wetland gardens with rare plants. Boat trips on Inner Broad. Tel: 01603 270449 www.fairhavengarden.co.uk

Hales Hall, Hales Green. About 2 miles *[3.2 km]* S of Loddon, off A146. Largest brick medieval barn in Britain, moated gardens, national collections of citrus, grapes and figs. Tel: 01508 548507 www.haleshall.com

Hoveton Hall Gardens. 1 mile *[1.6 km]* N of Wroxham on the A1151. Ten acres *[4 ha]* of garden in a woodland setting. Tel: 01603 782798 www.hovetonhallgardens.co.uk

Old Vicarage, East Ruston. 3 miles *[5.25 km]* N of Stalham off A149. Mediterranean, Dutch, walled gardens, tropical and Californian borders. Tel: 01692 650432 www.e-ruston-oldvicaragegardens.co.uk

Priory Maze and Gardens, Cromer Road, Beeston, Sheringham. Varied gardens with maze, pine walk, secret garden, wildflower meadow, ponds, stream and log cabin tearooms. Tel: 01263 822986 www.priorymazegardens.com

Raveningham Hall Gardens, Loddon. 6 miles *[9.5 km]* NW of Beccles off A146 on B1136. Plantsman's garden, walled kitchen garden, herb garden and orchard. Open from Easter to end of August. Tel: 01508 548152 www.raveningham.com

Sailing on Whitlingham Great Broad

Sheringham Park (NT), Upper Sheringham. Off A148. Mature mixed woodland and landscaped park designed in 1812 by Humphrey Repton. Tel: 01263 820550

Somerleyton. 6 miles *[9.5 km]* SW of Great Yarmouth off A143. Woodland walks, formal gardens, adventure playground, golf, pony rides, mini tractors, wellie trail and rowing and fishing on lake. Tel: 01493 488288 www.somerleyton.co.uk

Whitlingham Country Park, Whitlingham Lane, Trowse. Two new broads near Norwich surrounded by meadows and woodland. Pleasant walks, fishing platforms, beaches and water activities. Tel: 01603 632307 www.whitlinghamoec.co.uk

Information

Churches Conservation Trust Tel: 020 7213 0660 www.visitchurches.org.uk

English Heritage (EH) Tel: 0870 3331181 www.english-heritage.org.uk

National Gardens Scheme Tel: 01483 211535 www.ngs.org.uk

National Trust (NT) Tel: 0870 4584000 www.nationaltrust.org.uk

Norfolk Churches Trust Tel: 01603 767576 www.norfolk-churches.co.uk

Suffolk Historic Churches Trust Tel: 01787 883884. www.shct.org.uk

St Benet's Abbey

This ruined Benedictine Abbey stands close to the River Bure near Ludham. It has a derelict windpump built in its midst. Excavations show that the abbey walls once enclosed an area of 36 acres *[14.6 ha]*.

Mills and windpumps

Wind-powered drainage mills were used from the eighteenth century to lift water up from dykes draining the marshland into the embanked rivers. Early wooden smock mills and brick tower mills had scoop wheels with paddles and 'common sails', covered in cloth, that had to be stopped and turned by a long tail pole connected to the cap when the wind changed. Later mills had a fantail to turn sails into the wind automatically and adjustable wooden shutters to cope with strong gusts. Turbine pumps were introduced in the middle of the nineteenth century. Two surviving timber mills can be seen at How Hill: Boardman's Mill and Clayrack Mill, a hollow post mill driving a scoop wheel.

Dressing the sails of Herringfleet Mill

Mills to visit

Berney Arms Windmill (EH), Halvergate marshes. 3 miles *[4.75 km]* W of Great Yarmouth. Access from Berney Arms Halt, by boat or by footpath from Halvergate and Great Yarmouth. Late nineteenth-century marsh windmill. Built as a grinding mill, but used for drainage from the mid-1950s. Currently closed for conservation. Tel: 01799 522842

Boardman's Mill (WT), How Hill, near Ludham. 2 miles *[3.25 km]* SW of Potter Heigham, off A1062. Open-framed timber trestle drainage mill.

Herringfleet Mill. 1.2 miles *[2 km]* SE of St Olaves, off B1074. Built in 1820–30, a working drainage smock mill first restored in the 1950s. Circular walk from car park at Herringfleet Hills. Tel: 01473 583352

Horsey Windpump (NT), Horsey, alongside B1159 at Horsey Staithe. 2½ miles *[4 km]* NE of Potter Heigham. Four-storey windpump, built in 1912. Tel: 01284 747500

St Olaves Windpump. N of St Olaves. Footpath from the bridge. Key from Bridge Stores. Tel: 01493 488230

Stracey Arms Mill (WT). 3 miles *[4.75 km]* E of Acle between A47 and River Bure. Partly restored drainage pump. Free moorings.

Sutton Mill, Sutton. 1 mile *[1.6 km]* SE of Stalham off A149. Nine-storey corn-mill, museum of trade and domestic items. Tel: 01692 582926

Boardman's Mill, How Hill

Thurne Dyke Drainage Mill (WT), Thurne. W of village off A149. Restored drainage mill.

Information

English Heritage (EH) Tel: 01223 582700 www.english-heritage.org.uk

Norfolk Windmills Trust (WT) Tel: 01603 222705 www.norfolkwindmills.co.uk

National Trust (NT) Tel: 01263 738000 www.nationaltrust.org.uk

Suffolk Mills Group www.suffolkmills.org.uk

Museums

Several specialist museums are devoted to local trades and history. Others, including *Norwich Castle*, are listed under *Norwich*, *Great Yarmouth* and *Lowestoft*.

Beccles and District Museum, Ballygate. Tel: 01502 715722 www.becclesmuseum.org.uk

Broads Museum, Sutton. 1 mile *[1.6 km]* SE of Stalham off A149 at Sutton Mill. Domestic, trade and farm tools, local bygones. Tel: 01692 582926

Bungay Museum, Council Offices. Tel: 01986 892176 www.bungay-suffolk.co.uk

Cromer Museum (NMS), East Cottages, Tucker Street. Tel: 01263 513543

The Museum of the Broads, Poor's Staithe, Stalham. Man's effect on the Broads environment. Special events and demonstrations. Tel: 01692 581681 www.northnorfolk.org/museumofthebroads

Sheringham Museum, Station Road. Tel: 01263 822895 www.sheringhammuseum.co.uk

East Anglia Transport Museum

Transport and machinery

There are three working steam railways and large collections of other vehicles. Lifeboat houses at Cromer and Gorleston (see page 22) can also be visited, as can an aviation museum (see page 16).

Air Defence and Radar Museum (NMS), RAF Neatishead, near Horning. History of radar from 1935, Battle of Britain 1942 operations and cold war operations room. Tel: 01692 631485 www.radarmuseum.co.uk

Barton House Railway, Hartwell Road, Wroxham. Miniature passenger-carrying railway with some steam trains. Apr to Oct, third Sun of month. Tel: 01603 782470.

Bure Valley Railway. 9-mile *[14.5 km]* narrow-gauge steam railway between Wroxham and Aylsham. Tel: 01263 733858 www.bvrw.co.uk

Caister Castle Car Collection, West Caister. 2 miles *[3.25 km]* N of Great Yarmouth off A149. Tel: 01572 787251 www.greateryarmouth.co.uk

RNLI Henry Blogg Museum, No. 2 Boathouse, The Promenade, Cromer. Lifeboat house on pier. Tel: 01263 511294 www.cromerlifeboats.org.uk

East Anglia Transport Museum, Carlton Colville. Working historic buses, trolley buses and trams. Tel: 01502 518459 www.eatm.org.uk

Muckleburgh Collection, Weybourne. 3 miles *[4.75 km]* W of Sheringham on A149. Second World War vehicles, model ships. Tel: 01263 588210 www.muckleburgh.co.uk

North Norfolk Railway, Sheringham. Steam railway to Weybourne and Holt. Tel: 01263 820800 www.nnrailway.co.uk

Station 146 Control Tower, Seething airfield, 4 miles *[6.4 km]* W of Loddon off A146. Dedicated to 448th Bomb Group. www.seething.org.uk

Strumpshaw Hall Steam Museum. 7 miles *[11.25 km]* E of Norwich off A47. Working beam engines, fairground ride and narrow-gauge railway. Tel: 01603 714535

Toad Hole Cottage Museum (see page 10)

Boardman's Mill

This open-framed timber trestle mill on the River Ant at How Hill was built in about 1897. It has a miniature cap, sails and fantail. The mill originally drove a scoop wheel, and was improved in 1912 after serious local flooding. A turbine was installed in about 1927.

Museum services

Norfolk Museums Service (NMS) museums.norfolk.gov.uk

Suffolk Museums Service www.suffolkcc.gov.uk

Fun for children

There are lots of things for kids to do in the Broads – both on water and on land – from canoeing, sailing and cycling to discovering wildlife in nature reserves or an animal park, or feeding farm animals and handling pets. Swimming pools and beaches are not too far away and many of the attractions have a variety of different activities on offer. There are museums and working mills to visit and steam engines to ride behind.

Carnivals are celebrated at several seaside towns during the summer and in Norwich the Lord Mayor's Celebrations happen in the second weekend of July. Activity afternoons are organised in Norwich parks and in the large seaside resorts. There are multiplex cinemas and theatres in the main towns. Norwich has its own puppet theatre and Nutmeg Puppets regularly put on shows as part of the *Fun in the Broads* programme of events organised by the Broads Authority.

Pond dipping

Regular activities

Sailors at Thurne Dyke

Activity afternoons. KidZone, Norwich City Parks. Free fun in local parks. Tel: 01603 212126 www.norwich.gov.uk

Windsurfing, canoeing and sailing. Whitlingham Country Park, Whitlingham Lane, Trowse. Pay as you play. Tel: 01493 369840 www.nycsoutdooreducation.co.uk

Fun in the Broads, Broads Authority. Exciting and interesting things to do in the Broads from April to December. Published in *broadcaster* each year and available at *Broads Information Centres* (see page 8). www.broads-authority.gov.uk

Useful website: www.bbc.co.uk/norfolk/kids

Other attractions

These are just a few of the many attractions in the Broads region that offer a variety of different activities.

Inspire, Coslany Street, Norwich. The chance to try out lots of scientific exhibits. Tel: 01603 612612 www.inspirediscoverycentre.com

Rapt attention at the Museum of the Broads, Stalham

Norwich Puppet Theatre, St James, Whitefriars. Puppet shows for everyone. Tel: 01603 629921

Norwich Castle. This castle was built nine hundred years ago and there are guided tours of the battlements and dungeons. All kinds of treasures are on display – you can try hands-on exhibits, and check out models, video screens and computer animation. Tel: 01603 493625 museums.norfolk.gov.uk

A Nutmeg puppet meets her fans

Origins, The Forum, Norwich.
Explore the story of Norfolk over the last 2000 years with hands-on displays.
Tel: 01603 727950
www.originsnorwich.co.uk

Pettitts Animal Adventure Park, Camp Hill, Reedham. 6 miles *[9.5 km]* S of Acle off B1140. Amusement rides, adventure golf, Falabella horses, miniature monkeys, wallabies and pets. Tel: 01493 700094
www.pettittsadventurepark.co.uk

New Pleasurewood Hills American Theme Park, Corton. 2 miles *[3.2 km]* N of Lowestoft off A12. Rides and thrills for all the family. Tel: 01502 586000
www.pleasurewoodhills.com

Wroxham Barns, Tunstead Road, Hoveton. 1½ miles *[2.5 km]* N of Wroxham off B1354. Watch local craftsmen at work, enjoy the traditional family funfair and meet the animals on the junior farm.
Tel: 01603 783911
www.wroxham-barns.co.uk

Whirligig beetles

Gyrinidae

These beetles swim in circles on the surface of water as if they are dancing, using short hind legs that act like oars. They have eyes that can see above and below the water at the same time, and sensitive antennae that feel small movements in the water, helping them to prey on insects that have fallen in.

Annual events

January

Norwich Theatre Royal. Pantomime

End January-mid March

Norwich Visiting Writers' Festival, Centre for Creative and Performing Arts, UEA

March

Lowestoft Pancake Races, Shrove Tuesday

Easter

Blickling Park Craft Fair

Norwich French Market

April

Lowestoft Mind, Body and Spirit Market

May

Bungay May Day Races

Cromer Folk on the Pier www.folkonthepier.co.uk

Lowestoft French Market

Norfolk and Norwich Festival. Tel: 01603 877750 www.nnfestival.org.uk

Norfolk Open Studios. Tel: 01603 877750 www.nnfestival.org.uk/OpenStudios

Norwich King Street Festival

June

East Coast Regatta

Great Yarmouth Seafront Illuminations

Lowestoft Fish Fayre

Norwich 50/100 Bike Ride. Charity cycle ride of 100 or 50 miles *[160/80 km]*, Sun in June. www.bike-events.com

Oulton Broad Powerboat Racing. Most Thursdays 18.00.

Royal Norfolk Show, The Showground, Norwich. Last Wed and Thur in month. Tel: 01603 748931 www.royalnorfolkshow.co.uk

July

Beccles Carnival. Last weekend.

Blickling Hall Star Concerts. Third and fourth weekends.

Bungay Festival

Eastern Light Motorcycle Cavalcade, Norwich to Lowestoft to Great Yarmouth

Great Yarmouth Seafront Fireworks. Every Wednesday evening.

Lowestoft Seafront Air Festival

Norwich Lord Mayor's Celebrations. Five days of celebration.

Norwich Openstages. Wet weather hotline tel: 01603 212219

Oulton Broad Powerboat Racing. Most Thursdays 18.00.

Sandringham Flower Show

Sheringham Lobster Potty Festival. Early July.

Wherry sailings. Broads Authority

Worstead Festival. Last weekend in month. www.worstead.co.uk

August

Aylsham Show, Blickling Park. Late Bank Hol Mon.

Beccles Vintage Wooden Boat National Rally

Cromer Carnival. Mid Aug.

Great Yarmouth Festival of Bowls

Great Yarmouth Seafront Fireworks. Every Wednesday evening.

Lowestoft Carnival

Norwich City Parks KidZone. Activity afternoons, Wed, Thur 13.00–16.00.

Norwich OpenStages. Wet weather hotline tel: 01603 212219

Oulton Broad Powerboat Racing. Most Thurs 18.00.

Sheringham Carnival. Early Aug.

Wherry sailings. Broads Authority

September

Great Yarmouth Maritime Festival

Lowestoft Scores Race

Horning Water Carnival. First Sat of term. Tel: 01692 630498

Oulton Broad Powerboat racing. Most Thurs 18.00.

Sandringham Rainbow Craft Fair

End September-end November

Norwich Arthur Miller Centre International Literary Festival, UEA

October

Norwich Beer Festival, St Andrew's Hall. Last week in month. Tel: 01603 408856 www.norwichcamra.org.uk

Norwich City Ghost and Horror Walk. Adam and Eve pub. Tel: 01953 607262 www.norwich-ghost-walks.co.uk

Norwich French Market. First weekend.

Norwich Halloween Ghost Cruises, City Boats. Tel 01603 701701 www.cityboats.co.uk

November

Blickling Hall Behind the Scenes Tours. Early Nov.

East Coast Jazz Festival, Norwich Arts Centre. First two weeks. Tel: 01603 660352 www.norwichartscentre.co.uk

Great Yarmouth Christmas Fayre. Late Nov.

Norwich Sparks in the Parks, fireworks, Earlham Park

Norwich Christmas Lights. From mid Nov.

December

Bungay Christmas Street Fair

Lowestoft High Street Christmas Fayre

Norwich New Year's Eve, firework display

Norwich Theatre Royal. Pantomime

Note: *exact dates vary from year to year. See local press for details and other events.*

Information

Blickling Hall, National Trust. Tel: 01263 783049 www.nationaltrust.org.uk

Broads Authority. Tel: 01603 610734 www.broads-authority.gov.uk

Great Yarmouth. Area information. Tel: 01493 846345 ww.great-yarmouth.co.uk

Lowestoft. Area information. Tel: 01502 533600 www.visit-lowestoft.co.uk

North Norfolk. Area information. Tel: 01263 513811 www.northnorfolk.org

Norwich. City events. Tel: 01603 622233 www.norwich.gov.uk

Norwich Theatre Royal. Tel: 01603 630000 www.theatreroyalnorwich.co.uk

Sandringham Estate. Tel: 01553 612908 www.sandringhamestate.co.uk

University of East Anglia (UEA). Tel: 01603 456161 www.uea.ac.uk

Regattas and sailing fixtures

Sailing clubs throughout the Broads organise regattas and river races between April and September each year. For more details see the following websites:

Hickling Broad Sailing Club www.hicklingbroad.com

Norfolk and Suffolk Yachting Association www.thegreenbook.org.uk

Norfolk Broads Yacht Club, Wroxham Broad www.nbyc.co.uk

Norfolk Punt Sailing Club, Barton Broad www.puntclub.co.uk

Royal Yachting Association www.rya.org.uk

Waveney and Oulton Broad Yacht Club www.saileast.co.uk/wobyc

Competitors in the Three Rivers Race

Swallow

Hirundo rustica

Swallows can often be seen in summer swooping over areas of water to catch insects on the wing. The swallow is slim in shape with long tail streamers. It has a dark throat and rump with a pale underside. Swallows build cup-shaped nests from mud pellets, often under eaves of buildings.

The Broads Quality Charter

The Broads is a great place to relax and unwind. And what better way to enjoy the area than with great quality local food and warm hospitality?

From haute cuisine to pub grub, this guide's for you. It lists the best places to eat – they've all been carefully checked and tested for quality, and scored highly.

Most eateries in the Broads area were tested – but only the ones with the highest scores are listed here. Anonymous inspectors rated the establishments on food, service, hospitality and cleanliness. If they scored over 60% across the board then they attained membership of the Broads Quality Charter.

This year there's more than ever for you to choose from. You'll also find an increasing range of interesting local dishes.

The aim is to raise quality for everyone and to work with businesses and customers. We'd like to know what you think, so please get in touch with your feedback.

There's an increasing range of tasty local food on offer in the Broads – use this guide to seek it out and enjoy it.

Note: Changes in ownership may affect the Quality Charter status of eating-places. Check the Broads Authority website for up-to-date information: www.broads-authority.gov.uk

Eating places

Key to restaurant symbols

 toilet accessible

 mooring available

 local specialities

 guideline price

Acle

The Bridge Inn

Old Road, Acle tel: 01493 750288

  £1.95~19.95

Grumpy's Cottage Restaurant

23 Old Road, Acle tel: 01493 751111

 £3~15.75

Hermitage Restaurant & Public House

64 Old Road, Acle tel: 01493 750310

  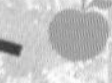 £7.95~16

Kings Head Inn

The Street, Acle tel: 01493 750204
kingsheadinnacle.co.uk

 £7.75~13.95

Beccles

The Bear and Bells

11 Old Market, Beccles, Suffolk
tel: 01502 712291 bearandbells.co.uk

  £5~15

Prezzo

9 Saltgate, Beccles tel: 01502 715036
prezzoplc.co.uk

 £2.75~8.95

The Swan House

By the Tower, Beccles tel: 01502 713474
swan-house.com

 £7~14.50

The Swan Inn

Swan Lane, Barnby tel: 01502 476646

 £3.95~19.95

Three Horseshoes

North Cove, Beccles tel: 01502 476601

  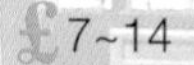 £7~14

Twyfords

Exchange Square, Beccles tel: 01502 710614

 £4.50~9

Waveney House Hotel

Puddingmoor, Beccles tel: 01502 712270
waveneyhousehotel.co.uk

    £4.50~17.95

Waveney Inn

Waveney River Centre, Burgh St Peter
tel: 01502 677599
martin-inns.co.uk

   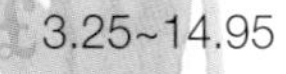 £3.25~14.95

Brundall

Lavender House Restaurant

39 The Street, Brundall tel: 01603 712215
thelavenderhouse.co.uk

 £36 a head (six courses)

Bungay

Earsham Street Café

13 Earsham Street tel: 01986 893103

 £4.50~14

Cantley

Reedcutters

Station Road, Cantley tel: 01493 701099
thereedcutter.co.uk

 £4.95~13.95

Chedgrave

The White Horse

5 Norwich Road, Chedgrave tel: 01508 520250

 £4.25~15.50

Coltishall

Andaman Orchid

41 Church Street, Coltishall
tel: 01603 736655

£3.95~14.95

The Kings Head Inn

26 Wroxham Road, Coltishall tel: 01603 737426

   £4.50~17.95

Norfolk Mead Hotel

Church Loke, Coltishall tel: 01603 737531
norfolkmead.co.uk

  £13.50~22

Red Lion Inn

77 Church Street, Coltishall tel: 01603 737402

 £8~15

Filby

The Filby Bridge Restaurant

Main Road, Filby tel: 01493 368142

  £6.25~21.95

Fritton

The Decoy Tavern

Beccles Road, Fritton tel: 01493 488277

 £3~9.25

Haddiscoe

The Crown Inn

The Street, Haddiscoe tel: 01502 677368
thecrownathaddiscoe.co.uk

 £7.95~16.95

Haddiscoe Tavern
at the Pampas Lodge

The Street, Haddiscoe tel: 01502 679918

  £6~11

Hickling

Greyhound Inn

The Green, Hickling tel: 01692 598306
greyhoundinn.com

 £2.95~12.50

Horning

Bure River Cottage Restaurant

27 Lower Street, Horning tel: 01692 631421

£4~26

Staithe and Willow Restaurant

16 Lower Street, Horning tel: 01692 630915
broads-norfolk.com

 £1.65~14.95

The Broads Quality Charter

Taps Restaurant
25 Lower Street, Horning tel: 01692 630219
tapsrestaurant.com
 12.95~17.95

Horstead

The Recruiting Sergeant
Norwich Road, Horstead tel: 01603 737077
recruitingsergeant.co.uk
  3.50~18

Hoveton

The Kings Head Hotel and Country Carvery
Station Road, Hoveton tel: 01603 782429
   2.75~7.95

Loddon

Rosy Lee's Tea Room
37 Bridge Street, Loddon tel: 01508 520204
  1.20~8.99

Ludham

Alfresco Tea Rooms
Norwich Road, Ludham tel: 01692 678384
 1.20~5.50

The Kings Arms
High Street, Ludham tel: 01692 678386
thekingsarmsludham.co.uk
  3.95~17.95

Neatishead

The White Horse Inn
The Street, Neatishead tel: 01692 630828
  3.95~17.95

Ye Olde Saddlery
The Street, Neatishead tel: 01692 630866
yeoldesaddlery.co.uk
  4.50~21.95

Oulton Broad

Broadland Holiday Village
Marsh Road, Oulton Broad
tel: 01502 500895 broadlandvillage.co.uk
  2.95~8.95

Crooked Barn Restaurant
at the Ivy House Country Hotel
Ivy Lane, Oulton Broad tel: 01502 501353
ivyhousecountryhotel.co.uk
  4.95~21.95

The Red Herring
152 Bridge Road, Oulton Broad, Lowestoft
tel: 01502 566499
  4~16

The Waveney Public House
132 Bridge Road, Oulton Broad, Lowestoft
tel: 01502 573940
   2~15.50

Wherry Hotel
Bridge Road, Oulton Broad tel: 01502 516845
elizabethhotels.co.uk
  8.50~14.95

Reedham

Reedham Ferry Inn
Ferry Road, Reedham tel: 01493 700429
archerstouringpark.co.uk
  3.95~19.95

Rockland St Mary

The New Inn
New Inn Hill, Rockland St Mary
tel: 01508 538403
  4.50~14.95

St Olaves

Priory Farm Restaurant
Beccles Road, St Olaves tel: 01493 488432
  3.25~15

Somerleyton

Dukes Head
Slugs Lane, Somerleyton tel: 01502 730281
somerleyton.co.uk
    4.50~15

South Walsham

Fairhaven Woodland and Water Garden
School Road, South Walsham
tel: 01603 270683

    £1.20~6

Stalham

Kingfisher Hotel
12 High Street, Stalham tel: 01692 581974
kingfisherhotel.co.uk

  £5.50~18

Wayford Bridge Hotel
Wayford Bridge, near Stalham
tel: 01692 582414 wayford-bridge-hotel.co.uk

  £7.95~15

Stokesby

Riverside Tearoom and Stores
The Green, Stokesby tel: 01493 750470

 £1.20~7.25

Thorpe St Andrew

Old Rectory Hotel
103 Yarmouth Road, Thorpe St Andrew, Norwich tel: 01603 700772
oldrectorynorwich.com

£23 (3 courses weekday) ~25 at weekends

River Garden Bar and Restaurant
36 Yarmouth Road, Thorpe St Andrew, Norwich
tel: 01603 703900 therivergarden.co.uk

    £4.35~15

Rushcutters
46 Yarmouth Road, Thorpe St Andrew, Norwich
tel: 01603 435403 thespiritgroup.com

   £2.95~14.95

Woodbastwick

Fur and Feather Inn
Slade Lane, Woodbastwick
tel: 01603 720003 thefurandfeatherinn.co.uk

  £3.75~13.50

Wroxham

The Bridge Restaurant
Norwich Road, Wroxham tel: 01603 783509

   £4.25~17.75

Canton Orient *Chinese Restaurant*
The Station, Wroxham tel: 01603 783939

£4.95~12

The Hotel Wroxham
The Bridge, Wroxham tel: 01603 782061
arlingtonhotelgroup.co.uk

   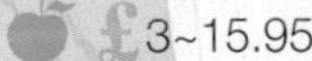 £3~15.95

The Rushcutters, Thorpe St Andrew, is one the many places to eat in the Norfolk Broads area which has achieved the Broads Quality Charter.

Public transport

Trains

Mainline services run from Norwich to Great Yarmouth and Lowestoft, known as the Wherry Lines, and to Sheringham - the section from Wroxham to the coast is the Bittern Line. Trains serve the following stations: Acle, Beccles, Berney Arms, Brundall, Brundall Gardens, Buckenham, Cantley, Haddiscoe, Lingwood, Oulton Broad, Reedham, Salhouse, Somerleyton and Worstead.

One Tel: 0845 600 7245 Minicom: 01603 630748/0845 6050600 www.onerailway.com

Bittern Line www.bittternline.com

Bure Valley Railway Narrow-gauge railway connecting Wroxham with Aylsham. Tel: 01263 733858 www.bvrw.co.uk

National Rail Enquiries Tel: 0845 7484950 www.nationalrail.co.uk

North Norfolk Railway The Poppy Line connects Sheringham and Holt. Tel: 01263 820800 Talking timetable: 01263 820808 www.nnrailway.co.uk

Wherry Lines www.wherrylines.org.uk

Buses

Most towns, villages and local attractions can be reached by bus, but not all services are regular, so it is wise to check timetables in advance through Traveline East Anglia.

Bure Valley Railway

General travel information

Broads Information Centres (see page 8).

Norfolk County Transport Guide, Passenger Transport Unit. Tel: 01603 223800

Traveline East Anglia Tel: 0871 200 2233 www.travelineeastanglia.org.uk

Visit Norfolk www.visitnorfolk.co.uk

Weather

Met Office Customer centre. Tel: 0870 900 0100

Regional weathercall telephone forecast. Tel: 09014 722058

Bus at the village of Martham

Weathercall seven-day forecast for Norfolk, Suffolk and Cambridgeshire. Tel: 09014 722058 www.metoffice.gov.uk

Local radio

BBC Radio Norfolk (95.1 and 104.4 FM) Tel: 01603 617411 www.bbc.co.uk/norfolk

BBC Radio Suffolk (95.5, 95.9, 103.9 and 104.6 FM) Tel: 01473 250000 www.bbc.co.uk/suffolk

Broadland 102 (102.4 FM) Tel: 01603 630621 www.radiobroadland.co.uk

Classic Gold Amber (1152 AM and DAB) www.classicgolddigital.co.uk

SGR (97.1 and 96.4 FM) Tel: 01473 461000 www.sgrfm.co.uk

The Beach (97.4 and 103.4 FM) Tel: 0845 345 1035 www.thebeach.co.uk

Maps of the area

GEOprojects The Broads

Jarrold Norfolk Broads

OS Landranger 133 (North East Norfolk)

OS Landranger 134 (Norwich and the Broads)

OS Explorer OL 40 (The Broads)

OS Touring Maps (Norfolk, Suffolk)

Walking and cycling

Walking

A network of footpaths and bridleways makes walking a pleasure. The Norfolk Coastal Path is part of the National Trail and there are two long-distance paths, the Weavers' Way and the Angles' Way, as well as shorter circular walks and nature trails.

Walking routes

Bittern Line Partnership.
Tel: 01263 711091 www.bitternline.com

Broadland District Council.
Out and About in Broadland.
Tel: 01263 733903 www.broadland.gov.uk

Broads Information Centres. Broads Walks, Bure Valley and Waveney Valley.
Tel: 01603 610734
www.broads-authority.gov.uk

Norfolk County Council. Long Distance Paths, Norfolk Circular Walks and Norfolk Parish Walks.
www.countrysideaccess.norfolk.gov.uk

National Trails Office.
www.nationaltrail.co.uk

The Norfolk Coast Millennium Access Project. Easy access paths.
www.norfolkcoastaonb.org.uk

Cycling

The rolling countryside is ideal for cycling. Bikes, including tandems, can be hired by the day or half-day, with free route maps. The Bittern Line and Bure Valley Railway encourage cyclists, and Anglia Railways offers a free recovery service. The Broads Hopper minibus, from Aylsham to Reedham via Wroxham and Acle, has a trailer for cycles.

National Cycle Network Route 1 runs through the area, forming part of the North Sea Cycle Route. The Norfolk Coast Cycleway – National Cycle Network Regional Route 30 – runs from King's Lynn to Great Yarmouth, and Route 30 continues from Lowestoft to Kings Lynn via Bungay.

Cycle routes

Bittern Line Partnership.
Tel: 01263 711091 www.bitternline.com

Broads Information Centres.
Broads Bike Trails.
Tel: 01603 610734/782281
www.broads-authority.gov.uk

National Cycle Routes/Sustrans.
www.sustrans.org.uk

Norfolk Coast Cycling Initiative.
www.cycle-norfolk.co.uk

North Sea Cycle Route
www.northsea-cycle.com

Wensum Valley Project. Wensum Valley Cycling Route Pack. Tel: 01362 861183

Bike hire

Bungay, Outney Meadow Caravan Park.
Tel: 01986 892338

Burgh St Peter, Waveney River Centre.
Tel: 01502 677343

Clippesby, Clippesby Hall.
Tel: 01493 367800

Hoveton, Broadland Cycle Hire,
The Rhond. Tel: 07887 480331

Ludham Bridge Boat Services.
Tel: 01692 630486

Stokesby, Riverside Tea Rooms and Stores. Tel: 01493 750470

Cycling code

- Take care when crossing and using main roads.
- Ride single file on busy roads – and never more than two abreast.
- Remember to signal before manoeuvring – other road users need to know.
- Keep to roads, bridleways and byways – footpaths are for pedestrians.
- Give pedestrians and horses plenty of room and slow down when you pass – horses can be easily startled, and may not hear you coming.
- Wear a safety helmet, and bright reflective clothing even in daylight.
- You must use lights after dark – it's important to be seen.

Peaceful walking country

Cycling along quiet lanes

Hiring a boat

Motor cruisers and yachts of from two to twelve berths can be hired from boatyards for a week or for longer or shorter breaks. Modern cruisers are comfortable and easy to handle. Boatyards give demonstrations to new skippers and supply manuals of useful information.

Motor launches can be hired by the hour, half-day or day from many boatyards. Electric dayboats, sailing dinghies, rowboats, canoes and windsurfers are also available in some yards. For boatyards see *Rivers and Broads* section.

An electric dayboat

Booking agencies

Blakes Holiday Boating,
Holiday Cottages Group, Spring Mill, Stoneybank Road, Earby, Barnnoldswick, Lancashire BB94 0AA.
Tel: 0870 2202498 www.blakes.co.uk

Hoseasons Holidays Ltd, Lowestoft NR32 2LW. Tel: 01502 502588
www.hoseasons.co.uk

Paddling our canoe

Canoe hire centres

Canadian canoes hold three adults or a family. Buoyancy aids and waterproof rucksacks are supplied, with advice on safety and suitable routes.

Bungay, Outney Meadow Caravan Park.
Tel: 01986 892338

Burgh St Peter, Waveney River Centre.
Tel: 01502 677343

Geldeston, Rowan Craft.
Tel: 01508 518208

Wayford Bridge, Bank Dayboats.
Tel: 01692 582457

Whitlingham Country Park.
Tel: 01603 632307

Wroxham, Barnes Brinkcraft,
Riverside Road. Tel: 01603 782625

Tide tables

The Broads waterways are tidal.
Tables are calculated each year to help navigators plan their journeys. The tide ebbs and flows twice in each lunar day – the height is governed by the moon and weather. The flow continues for about five hours; the ebb for seven hours. Water speed varies from ½ to 5 mph *[0.8–8 kph]*, according to the distance from the sea.

The times of tides also depend on the distance inland. Tables show low water at Great Yarmouth Yacht Station, so these figures need to be adjusted (see navigation details in *Rivers and Broads*). High water is about six hours before and after low water. The tables allow for British Summer Time.

The current at Great Yarmouth continues to flow outwards after low water. Slack water, at the turn of a tide, is usually about 30 minutes to 1 hour 15 minutes later. Manoeuvring at Yarmouth is easier at this time.

For tide tables see:
www.hamiltonpublications.com
www.norfolkbroads.com

The Three Rivers Race

Boating for all

Some cruisers are suitable for people with limited mobility and the following organisations provide access to boats with specially designed facilities.

Boat trips

Broadland Passenger Craft, Wroxham/Hoveton. Large passenger boat, space for five wheelchair users, accessible toilet. Tel: 01603 782527

A trip on Ra at Barton Broad

Broads Authority, Barton Broad. Guided trips aboard the open solar-powered *Ra* for 12 passengers. Access ramp. Tel: 01603 782281

Broads Tours, Wroxham. Space for up to eight wheelchair users (manual), wide access toilets. Tel: 01603 782207 www.broads.co.uk

City Boats, Norwich. Trips and ferry service to Whitlingham Country Park, space for up to four wheelchair users. Tel: 01603 701701 www.cityboats.co.uk

George Smith and Sons, The Rhond, Hoveton. Passenger boat with wide access toilet. Tel: 01603 782527 www.dayboathire.com

Southern Comfort, Horning. Up to six wheelchair users on scheduled trips or 20 for private parties. Tel: 01692 630262

Dayboats

In the following locations, wheelchair-accessible boats can be hired directly.

Broads Authority, Eels Foot Inn, Ormesby St Michael. Wheelyboat with access for one wheelchair user. Tel: 01493 730342

King Line, Ferry Road, Horning. Self-drive electric launch with electric lift for wheelchairs and remote control steering. Seats 11 people, takes up to three wheelchairs, toilet on board. Tel: 01692 630297 www.norfolk-broads.co.uk

Princess Cruisers, Loddon. Wheelyboat, with access ramp and electric motor, takes three people including one wheelchair. Tel: 01508 520353

Somerleyton, Fritton. Wheelyboat. Tel: 01493 488288 www.somerleyton.co.uk

Waveney Stardust, Beccles. Single-deck cruiser with hydraulic lift for wheelchair users and people with other disabilities, for up to 12 passengers, galley and toilet. Skipper included. Tel: 07817 920502 www.waveneystardust.co.uk

Sailing with the Nancy Oldfield Trust

Boating centres and holiday hire

Camelot Craft, Hoveton. Sailing for visually impaired and blind. Tel: 01603 783096 www.norfolksailingschool.co.uk/camelot

Nancy Oldfield Trust, Neatishead. Motor cruising, sailing, canoeing and kayaking for all. Also birdwatching and fishing. Day activities, holidays and courses. Facilities on land and afloat, including for carers. One cruiser yacht and two motor cruisers, with wheelchair access, for trips and holidays. Tel: 01692 630572 www.nancyoldfield.org.uk

Peter Le Marchant Trust, at Brooms of Brundall. Tel: 01509 265590 www.peterlemarchanttrust.co.uk

Ragged Robin

Lychnis flos-cuculi

This common wild plant thrives in marshes and damp meadows, growing to 70 cm *[2 ft 3 in]* high. It has a pinkish tinge to its stem and leaves and produces straggly pink flowers from April to July.

Safety aboard

Boating is safe for those who are sensible, but accidents involve the added danger of deep water, so extra care is needed – particularly with children, who should wear lifejackets and never be left unwatched. Remember too that alcohol can affect our judgement and sense of balance on land, let alone on water!

Pass behind a sailing craft

Rules of the river

- Keep to the right side of the river.
- Give way to sailing craft
  – always pass behind them.
- Give way to commercial vessels
  – they are slow to manoeuvre.
- Watch the speed limits
  – speed checks can lead to fines.
- Keep away from any boat being towed.
- Always moor before dusk.

Lifejackets help to keep us all safe

Personal safety

- Wear a lifejacket – you'll have a better chance if you do fall in.
- Wear non-slip shoes and use handrails – decks are slippery when wet.
- To avoid crushing, don't hang arms or legs over the side at any time.
- Don't jump the gap between boat and bank when mooring – this is where most injuries occur.
- Never ride in a dinghy while it is being towed.
- Bridges – mind your head.
- Don't swim
  – there are many unseen dangers.

Mooring

- Look for spots with wooden quay headings and posts for the ropes.
- Moor parallel to the bank – except where it is permitted to moor stern first.
- Moor facing the current, or the wind if that is stronger – for greater control whilst approaching the bank.
- Slacken ropes to allow for the rise and fall of the tide – see the navigation notes in the *Rivers and broads* section.
- Do not moor to marker buoys or posts – they are not strong and need to be visible to other boats.
- Keep out of the reeds
  – they are easily damaged.

Man overboard

- Avoid getting in the water yourself
  – it's dangerous and you're likely to be more help out of the water.
- Throw a lifebuoy or rope to within reach, taking care not to hit the person in the water and keeping a secure hold on the other end.
- Or hold out a boathook to the person with one hand and take a firm grip on the boat with the other.
- Use a dinghy if available
  – remember your lifejacket.
- If you must go in to rescue an unconscious person, take off shoes and bulky clothing – so they won't weigh you down.
- Don't go in after a dog
  – dogs often rescue themselves, but owners frequently can't!

If the person appears unconscious:

- Call 999.
  Remember to think where you are.
- Try to revive the person immediately.

Bridges

Some Broads bridges are so low, they can only be navigated at low tide – see the table of bridge heights on the inside back cover. Watch out for warning signs.

Navigation rangers are there to help

- Check the water-height gauge against the height of your boat.
- Lower canopies, windscreens and masts.
- Check everyone is inside the boat – below cabin-top level.
- Check nothing is coming the other way. Give a long blast on the horn. Generally the boat travelling with the current has the right of way.
- Pass through with enough speed to keep control. If you are too slow, the wind or tide may pull you into the bridge walls.
- If you need to, fend off with a boat hook, not hands or feet.
- Slow down when you are through.
- Check weather and tide conditions again on your way back – things may have changed.

Bridge pilots

Potter Heigham This bridge is dangerous, because of the changes in the river level between high and low tides. The pilot service, which must be used by all hire craft, is available 8.30–18.00, depending on the tide and weather conditions, from Phoenix Fleet boat yard.
Tel: 01692 670460

Wroxham Bridge Pilot service available 9.00–17.00 from Broads Boats.
Tel: 01603 783043

Bridges

Some bridges are low and dangerous. Always check the tides and the height of your boat before trying to pass through. Use the bridge pilot at Potter Heigham, and at Wroxham if you are in any doubt.

Don't swim!

Mind your head!

Don't jump!

River Bure Coltishall to Wroxham

The River Bure rises near Melton Constable and is navigable for 31½ miles *[50 km]* from Coltishall Lock to Great Yarmouth, where it joins the River Yare and flows out into the North Sea. It is tidal as far as Wroxham. The Rivers Ant and Thurne join the Bure between Horning and Acle.

The New Rising Sun at Coltishall Common

Coltishall

The historic settlement of Coltishall once had a local brewery and large wherries were built in the boatyards here. The village has substantial houses from the seventeenth and later centuries, and a thatched fourteenth-century church with two Saxon windows. Coltishall is 7 miles *[11 km]* north of Norwich on the B1150.

The antiques shops are well worth exploring, and there is a good range of facilities, including a supermarket, pharmacy, launderette, restaurants and a petrol station.

There are good moorings at Coltishall Common – a pleasant picnic area, with toilets, electric recharging point and a phone nearby. The Norfolk Mead Hotel, near the lock, has moorings for patrons.

Pubs

King's Head, Wroxham Road. Tel: 01603 737426

The Railway Tavern, Station Road. Tel: 01603 738316

The Recruiting Sergeant, Norwich Road, Horstead. Tel: 01603 737077

The Red Lion, Church Street. Tel: 01603 737402

New Rising Sun, Wroxham Road. Tel: 01603 737440

The village of Belaugh

Belaugh

The river between Coltishall and Belaugh, a distance of 1½ miles *[2.4 km]*, bends around marshes and fishing is good here. Belaugh is an attractive cluster of houses, dominated by the tower of the fifteenth-century church of St Peter, which has its own mooring and is open daily. The public staithe has moorings for two boats and there is a phone at the top of the hill.

Belaugh to Wroxham

The river passes through woodland and negotiates a large loop before reaching Wroxham, a total distance of 3½ miles *[5.6 km]*. There is a small staithe with free mooring on the eastern bank, just past the private Belaugh Broad. On the hill above is the fifteenth-century St Mary's Church, Wroxham. About a mile further, on the other bank, is a convenient staithe, where masts and canopies can be lowered before passing under the railway and road bridges at Wroxham. On the facing side are two entrances to Bridge Broad.

Good shopping at Hoveton

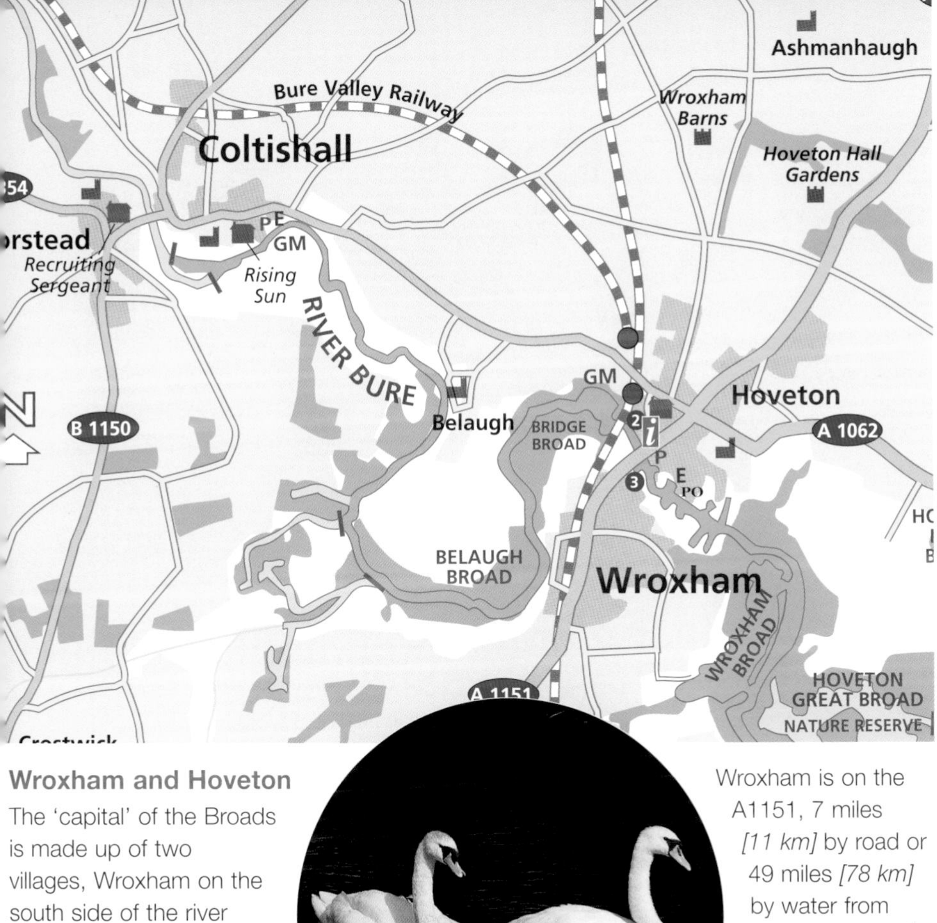

Wroxham and Hoveton

The 'capital' of the Broads is made up of two villages, Wroxham on the south side of the river and Hoveton St John on the north. A small boatyard was set up at Wroxham Bridge in 1880 and this has always been one of the main centres for Broads holidays. It is an excellent shopping centre with all kinds of useful facilities, including restaurants, major clearing banks, Roys – probably the largest village store in the country – a launderette, fishing tackle shop and yacht chandlers.

Mute swans *Cygnus olor*

Wroxham is on the A1151, 7 miles *[11 km]* by road or 49 miles *[78 km]* by water from Norwich and 19½ miles *[31 km]* by road or 25½ miles *[41 km]* by water from Great Yarmouth. It is on the mainline railway between Norwich and Sheringham, and the narrow-gauge *Bure Valley Railway* (see page 29) runs for 9 miles *[14.5 km]* to Aylsham, a pleasant market town close to *Blickling Hall* (see page 26). Beside the railway track is the Bure Valley Path. Request halts at Brampton, Buxton and Coltishall make it possible to mix walking or cycling with a train journey, and the trains also take wheelchairs.

There are regular buses to Norwich and local services to Horning, Ludham, Potter Heigham, Stalham and to Sea Palling, where clean sandy beaches can be found beyond the high dunes.

Wroxham Barns, 1½ miles *[2.4 km]* N off the B1354 Tunstead Road, has craft workshops, a tearoom and a junior farm (see page 25). Also within easy reach, one mile *[1.6 km]* north on the A1151, are *Hoveton Hall Gardens* (see page 27). *Barton House Railway*, a miniature railway, is just downstream from the village centre on the right bank (see page 29).

Broads Information Centre, Station Road. Tel: 01603 782281.

Navigation and moorings

The tide does not run fast, and is light above the railway bridge. Rise and fall is 10–15 cm *[4–6 in]*. High and low water are about five hours later than at Great Yarmouth Yacht Station. The best time for motor craft to leave for Great Yarmouth and down river is just after high water. This is a busy part of the river and a pilot is available for negotiating the road bridge (see *Wroxham Launch Hire*, below).

There are moorings above and below the bridge, at Blakes Staithe and at many boatyards, and patrons of the King's Head and Hotel Wroxham may use their moorings.

Barn owl
Tyto alba

Sometimes seen in daylight when feeding its young, this striking owl has a white heart-shaped facial disc. Its upper body is light grey with scattered pale spots and buff markings on the feathers. The underparts are white with a few black spots. Barn owls prey on small rodents in open farmland, and nest in barns and ruins.

River Bure Coltishall to Wroxham

Wroxham Bridge

Boatyards and cottages

Barnes Brinkcraft, Riverside Road, Hoveton. Cruisers, canoes, dayboats, houses. Tel: 01603 782625 www.barnesbrinkcraft.co.uk

PO WC

Broads Tours and Faircraft Loynes, The Bridge, Wroxham. Cruisers, cottages, electric and diesel dayboats, passenger craft. Tel: 01603 782207 www.broads.co.uk

PO WC

Camelot Craft, The Rhond, Hoveton. Family sailing tuition, no upper age. Yachts and sailing craft, bikes. Yacht repairs. Tel: 01603 783096 www.norfolksailingschool.co.uk/camelot

E

Connoisseur, Wroxham. Cruisers. Tel: 01603 782472 www.connoisseurboating.co.uk

PO WC

Fineway Cruisers, Riverside Road, Hoveton. Cruisers, electric and diesel dayboats. Tel: 01603 782309 www.finewayleisure.co.uk

PO WC

George Smith and Sons, The Rhond, Hoveton. Day and short-break cruisers, passenger craft with disabled facilities. Tel: 01603 782527 www.dayboathire.com

Moore and Co., Staitheway Road, Wroxham. Cruisers, cottages. Tel: 01603 783311 www.boatingholidays.co.uk

PO WC

Royall and Son, Riverside Road, Hoveton. Cruisers, dayboats. Tel: 01603 782743

PO WC

Sabena Marine, Marsh Road, Hoveton. Cruisers. Tel: 01603 782552 www.sabenamarine.co.uk

PO WC

Summercraft, Bimbelow Road, Hoveton. Cruisers, cottages with dayboats. Tel: 0870 4059479 www.hoseasons.co.uk

PO WC

Wroxham Launch Hire, The Bridge, Hoveton. Dayboats, fishing boats, rowboats, picnic boats, pilotage, river trips. Tel: 01603 783043

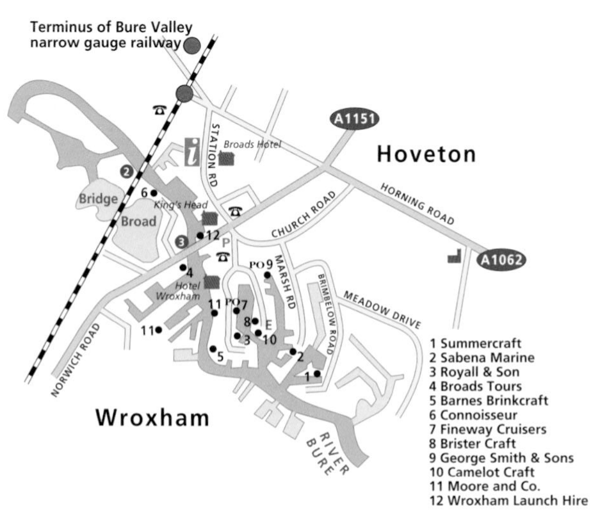

Cycle hire

Broadland Cycle Hire, The Rhond. Tel: 07887 480331

Huff & Puff Cycle Hire, Wroxham and Aylsham stations. Tel: 0788 132909

Pub *King's Head Hotel*, Station Road, Hoveton. Tel: 01603 782429

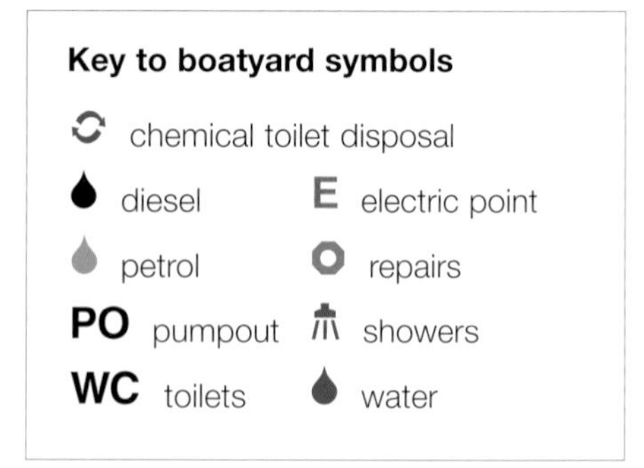

Wroxham Regatta

Wroxham Broad

A mile *[1.6 km]* below Wroxham, on the south side of the river, is an entrance to Wroxham Broad, a gap in the strip of land separating the broad from the river. The broad is home to a local sailing club. Landing is not permitted, but mooring or fishing mid-broad is allowed for a small fee. Racing takes place most weekends during the summer.

Norfolk Broads Yacht Club.
www.nbyc.co.uk

Hoveton Great Broad

About a mile *[1.6 km]* further on the northern bank is a mooring for visitors to Hoveton Great Broad nature trail, which is open during the summer. A boardwalk of ½ mile *[800 m]* leads across marshy ground with a view of this unique habitat.

Salhouse

In the opposite bank are the two entrances to Salhouse Broad. There is a charge for fishing and for mooring, but this is ideal for a quiet stop, with good moorings and a pleasant grassy bank. A noticeboard gives details of Salhouse, about ½ mile *[800 m]* from the broad.

A footpath beside ancient oaks links the broad with an unobtrusive car park, where there are toilets and rubbish bins. The village, with post office and phone, is to the right. A brisk 10-minute walk to the left is the *Fur and Feather Inn* at Woodbastwick (see below).

To look round the squat-towered fourteenth-century All Saints Church, on the Wroxham road, tel: 01603 721110 or 721912.

Salhouse Broad

Buses run to Norwich and to Wroxham. The station, with train service to Norwich and north to Sheringham, is 2½ miles *[4 km]* from the village.

Pubs

Bell Inn, Lower Street. Tel: 01603 721141

The Lodge Country House, Vicarage Road. Tel: 01603 782828

Salhouse Broad to Horning

Downriver on the south side is the private Woodbastwick Staithe and a long reach to Dydler's Mill, now a private house. The wooded banks change to flat fenland, and a dyke to the north leads to Hoveton Little Broad – or Black Horse Broad, as it is known locally – which is open for cruising in summer. No fishing or mooring is allowed.

Lower Street, Horning

Horning

Horning probably dates from Roman times and was important during the Middle Ages, when St Benedict's Church was built. Later there were malting houses, and

Pike

Esox lucius

The pike has a cylindrical body with its dorsal fin close to the tail fin. Its back is grey-green or brownish, the greenish sides have yellow spots or stripes and the belly is white with light grey spots. A predatory fish, it feeds on other fish and their fry.

River Bure Wroxham to Ant Mouth

the staithe was busy with wherries. Now Horning is a holiday centre, with a variety of shops.

The village stretches along the Bure, with its main street, Lower Street, parallel to the river. By water it is 4 miles *[6.4 km]* from Wroxham and 20½ miles *[33 km]* from Great Yarmouth Yacht Station. By road it is 2½ miles *[4 km]* from Wroxham and 17 miles *[27 km]* from Great Yarmouth. The nearest rail station is at Wroxham, and buses run to Wroxham and Norwich, and infrequently to Great Yarmouth.

Horning Sailing Club, the base in winter for the Snowflakes Club, is at the western end of the village. Races are held along the river towards Wroxham and the annual Three Rivers Race starts at Horning. The *Southern Comfort* paddleboat, built for Broads trips in 1974, departs from a quay next to the Swan Inn. Horning is also popular in winter for pike fishing. *The Air Defence and Radar Museum* is just north of Horning (see page 29).

Horning Ferry and boatyards

Navigation and moorings

A steady current runs through Horning, and the rise and fall of the tide is from 15 to 23 cm *[6–9 in]*. High and low water are about four hours later than at Great Yarmouth Yacht Station. The best time for craft to leave down river is one hour after high water.

The public staithe is next to the village green; there are other moorings at the pubs, hotels and boatyards and on the opposite bank for those with a dinghy.

Southern Comfort *from Ranworth church*

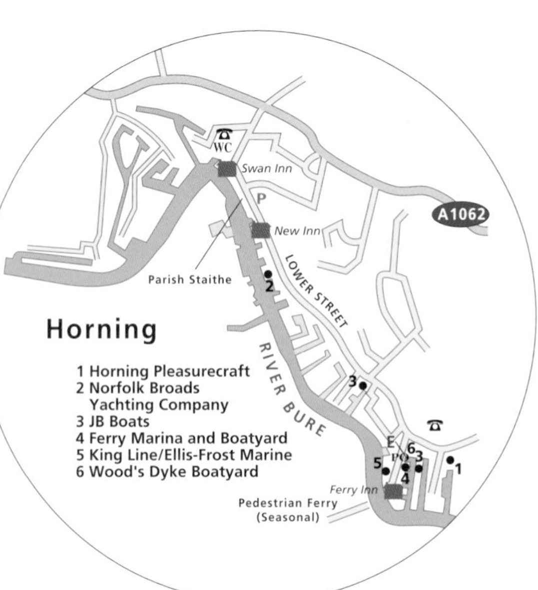

Boatyards, cottages and activities

Many of the riverside chalets are available through *Blakes* and *Hoseasons* (see page 40).

Ferry Marina and Boatyard, Ferry Road. Day launches, chalets, leisure centre. Tel: 01692 631111 www.ferry-marina.co.uk
♦ E ♦ ○ PO WC ♦

Horning Pleasurecraft, Ferry View Estate. Cruisers. Tel: 01692 582277 www.newhorizonhols.com ♦ PO ♦

Horning Sailing Club. www.horningsc.co.uk

JB Boats, Lower Street. Dayboats, dinghies and cottage. Tel: 01692 631411 www.about-norfolk.com/jbboats

King Line, Ferry Road. Rowboats, sailing dinghies, electric dayboat with space for three wheelchairs and attendants,

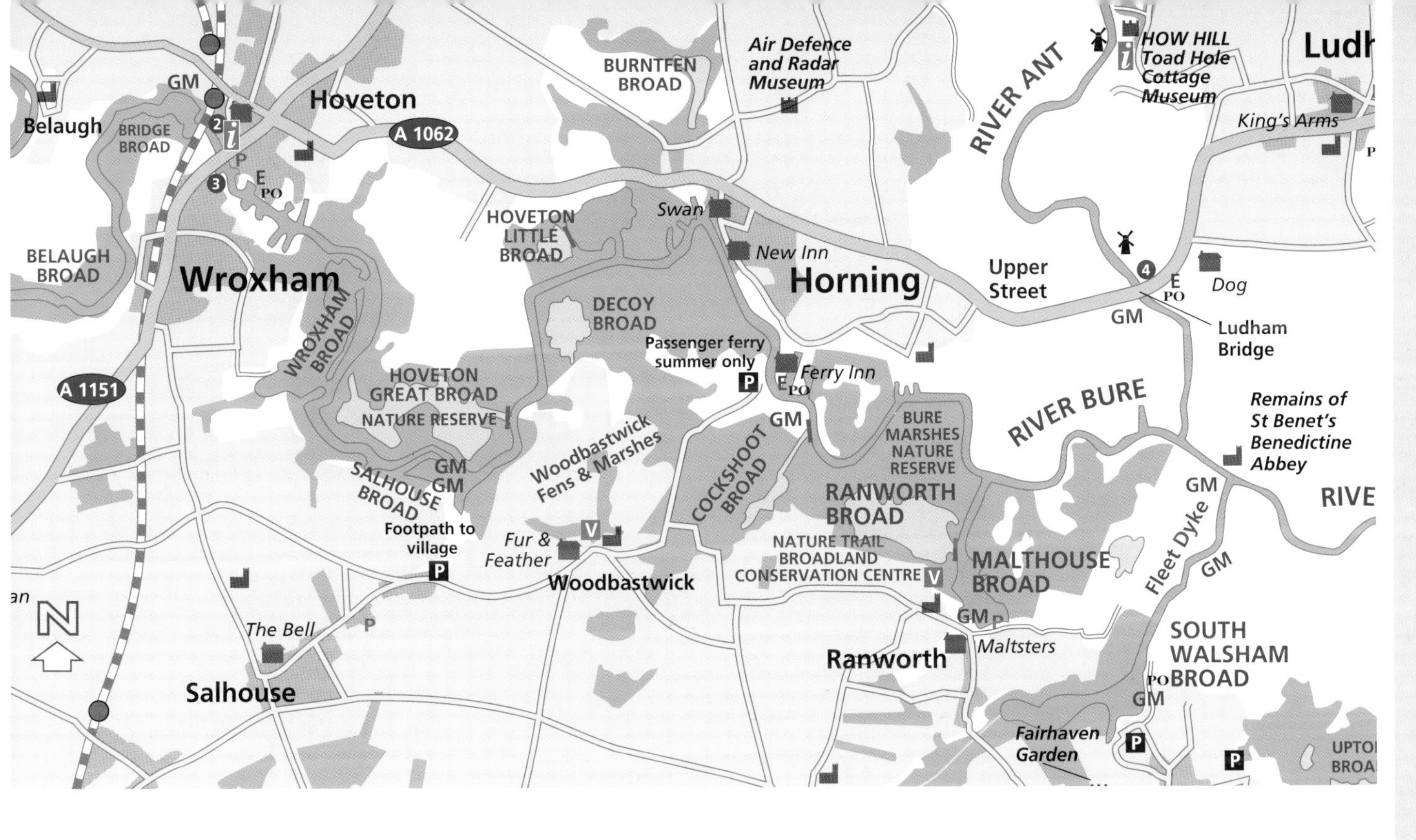

accessible holiday lodges. Tel: 01692 630297 www.norfolk-broads.co.uk

Norfolk Broads Yachting Company, Lower Street. Sailing yachts, dayboats, dinghies, rowing boats. Tel: 01692 631330 www.nbyco.com **PO WC**

Southern Comfort. Tel: 01692 630262 www.southern-comfort.co.uk

Woods Dyke Boatyard, School Road. Cruisers, rowboats, sailing dinghies, passenger ferry. Tel: 01692 630461 www.woodsdyke-boatyard.co.uk **PO WC**

Pubs

Ferry Inn, Ferry Road. Tel: 01692 630259

The New Inn, Lower Road. Tel: 01692 631223

Swan Inn, Lower Street. Tel: 01692 630316

Horning Ferry

There has been a river crossing here for over a thousand years. A passenger ferry that also carries bikes operates hourly from Woods Dyke Boatyard on weekdays in summer. The southern bank, which is popular with fishermen, can also be reached from Woodbastwick. A boardwalk leads to *Cockshoot Broad* from the car park (see page 9).

The Ferry Inn has a good length of quay, with no mooring charge during the day. Dykes lead to the boatyards. There are good moorings in Cockshoot Dyke and other moorings ½ mile *[800 m]* further on.

Cockshoot Broad

Cockshoot Broad is part of the Bure Marshes National Nature Reserve. A boardwalk leads from the car park for ¾ mile *[1.2 km]* along Cockshoot Dyke to the edge of the broad, which was cut off

Yellow flag iris
Iris pseudacorus

This aquatic plant brings a touch of colour in May and June. It can be seen at the water edges and in reedbeds throughout the Broads area.

from the river by a dam and suction-dredged in 1982. The resulting clear water has led to a recovery in water plants and wildlife. A bird hide overlooks the broad.

Woodbastwick

The village, about 1¼ miles *[2 km]* south of the river, has a pretty village green with a thatched pumphouse and nearby phone. The Church of St Fabian and St Sebastian, which is open to visitors, is in the Decorated style and is also thatched. The pub is run by a brewery, which also has a shop and visitor centre, and runs pre-booked group tours.

Pub and brewery

The Fur and Feather Inn, Slad Lane.
Tel: 01603 720003

Woodforde Broadland Brewery.
Tel: 01603 720353/722218
www.woodfordes.co.uk

Cockshoot Dyke to Ranworth

The church to the north is St Benedict's, Horning, and there are moorings on the river and in Vicarage Dyke. On the southern side, the river passes the Bure Marshes nature reserve, with views of St Helen's Church at Ranworth. The entrance to Ranworth Dyke is ¾ mile *[1.2 km]* downstream. The dyke, which leads to Ranworth and Malthouse Broads, is popular for fishing in early morning and evening.

Ranworth

Ranworth is the site of the *Broads Wildlife Centre* (see page 9) and Ranworth Broad itself is closed to craft. The staithe and moorings are in Malthouse Broad. Visitors to the centre can take the electric ferry, *Helen*, from the staithe or turn right along the path to the ¼-mile *[400 m]* boardwalk through carr woodland. The thatched centre has a wildlife exhibition and birdwatching gallery. Ranworth also has a pub, a phone and a post office with provisions shop and coffee shop.

There are magnificent views from the tower of *St Helen's Church* (see page 26), stretching for 15 miles *[24 km]* on a clear day and including *Horsey Windpump* (see page 28) and five broads. This church, the 'Cathedral of the Broads', has an exquisitely illuminated service book on display and the most complete medieval painted screen in the country. It is open daily and there is a welcoming tea shop in the churchyard.

St Helen's Church, Ranworth

Broads Information Centre, The Staithe.
Tel: 01603 270453

Broads Wildlife Centre at Ranworth

Moorings

Boats may tie up for a fee on the left bank of Malthouse Broad, although there is no access to the village. Alternatively craft with dinghies may anchor in the centre with mudweights. Mooring at the staithe itself is free, stern-on and limited, but some space is reserved for dayboats. There are toilets, litter containers and water is available.

Pub

The Maltsters, The Hill.
Tel: 01603 270241

Ant Mouth

From Ranworth Dyke the River Bure winds left and right to reach a private dyke on the left leading to Horning Hall. Beside it stands the chapel of the ancient Hospital of St James, now a barn, which was connected with St Benet's Abbey, and across the marshes ahead are the ruins of the Benedictine abbey itself. On the left almost immediately is the mouth of the River Ant.

River Ant Ant Mouth to Dilham

The River Ant rises near North Walsham and flows into the Bure just above St Benet's Abbey. The river is narrow, shallow and twisting, and can be busy, but it is possible to navigate for 8¾ miles *[14 km]* as far as Dilham. The tide is felt up to Barton Broad, where the rise and fall is 15 cm *[6 in]*.

Ludham Bridge

About a mile *[1.6 km]* above where the Ant joins the Bure and 3½ miles *[5.6 km]* south of Barton Broad is Ludham Bridge, which carries the A1062 Horning to Ludham road. Beside the bridge are a provisions and gift shop, restaurant, phone, chandlers and craft shops – and toilets and a pub are nearby.

Navigation and moorings

Power craft must slow down when passing under the bridge and sound their horns. The headroom at average high tide is 2.6 m *[8 ft 6 in]* and there is a rise and fall of tide of 17.5 to 23 cm *[7–9 in]*. High and low water are about 3 hours 40 minutes after Great Yarmouth Yacht Station. There are moorings on both banks.

Boatyard

Ludham Bridge Boat Services. Wildlife tours on electric launch to Ranworth, cycle hire centre, dayboats, general boatyard services, bottled gases. Tel: 01692 630486 www.ludhambridgeboats.co.uk

Pub

The Dog Inn, Johnsons Street.
Tel: 01692 630321

Toad Hole Cottage, How Hill

How Hill

A loop to the left in the river needs caution, before passing Turf Fen Windpump on the left and arriving at *How Hill* nature reserve (see page 10). Toad Hole Cottage Museum is furnished as in 1900. There are moorings on the right bank close to *Boardman's Mill*, and a little further on is *Clayrack Mill* (see page 28).

Broads Information Centre, *Toad Hole Cottage Museum* and *Electric Eel* water trail. Tel: 01692 678763

Cyclists rest at Irstead staithe

Irstead

On the right there are good moorings, but no access to Cromes Broad Dyke. The river winds to the left and narrows at Irstead staithe. A thatched cottage overlooks the green and the nearby fourteenth-century church is also thatched.

Barton Broad

The river opens out into Barton Broad, a nature reserve and home to the Norfolk Punt Club and *Nancy Oldfield Trust* (see page 41). Fenced fish-proof areas allow the population of *Daphnia* (water fleas) to thrive and so control the level of algae.

The Broads Authority car park has toilets and is the start of a footpath to the boardwalk and viewing platform in Herons' Carr. Solar-powered *Ra* departs from nearby Gay's Staithe. A disabled car park is close to the boardwalk on Irstead Road.

Navigation and moorings

There are moorings at Gay's Staithe, on the left near the entrance to Lime Kiln Dyke, and at Neatishead Staithe at the head of the dyke. When crossing the broad, keep to the marked channels and right of Pleasure Hill Island. At the northern end, a channel leads west to Barton Turf, where there are moorings at the staithe and on Paddy's Lane.

Kingfisher

Alcedo attis

This small bird is fast in flight, but can be glimpsed as a flash of colour on Broadland rivers. It has a bright orange-red breast and greeny-blue back and a distinctive black pointed beak. Kingfishers feed on small fish and insects.

River Ant Ant Mouth to Dilham

Boating and activities

Norfolk Punt Club. www.puntclub.co.uk

Nancy Oldfield Trust. Tel: 01692 630572 www.nancyoldfield.co.uk

Ra Gay's Staithe. Tel: 01692 670779

Neatishead

Neatishead is an attractive village with a general store, restaurant and pub. To the south towards Horning is the *Air Defence and Radar Museum* (see page 29), and *Willow Farm Flowers Dried Flower Centre* is about one mile *[1.6 km]* southwest, at Cangate (see page 25).

Pub

The White Horse, The Street. Tel: 01692 630828

Sutton staithe

Sutton

The river upstream of Barton Broad is narrow and heavily wooded. Craft bound for Sutton and Stalham bear right at a signposted junction. Sutton staithe, with good moorings and a pub, lies at the eastern end of Sutton Broad. The village, on the far side of A149, has a general shop with post office, a phone, an aquatic nursery and a pottery. *Sutton Mill* is about one mile *[1.6 km]* E (see page 28).

Boatyard and cottages

Sutton Staithe Boat Yard. Canoe hire centre, electric dayboats, dinghies, cycle hire, riverside cottages. Tel: 01692 581653 www.suttonstaitheleisure.co.uk

♦ O PO ♦

Pub *Sutton Staithe Hotel*, Sutton. Tel: 01692 580244

Stalham

Stalham is a good centre for exploring the northern Broads, and only 4 miles *[6.4 km]* from the nearest sandy beach. The typical country-town High Street has a range of shops and other facilities, plus a nearby supermarket with petrol station. The pay and display car park has information boards. A small market operates on Tuesdays and the town hall hosts various regular sales, including a farmers' market on alternate Saturdays. The tiny Coronation Fire Engine House is on the High Street. The *Museum of the Broads*, at Poor's Staithe, chronicles man's effect upon the Broadland environment (see page 29). The public staithe at the end of the dyke has information about the five-mile circular parish walk.

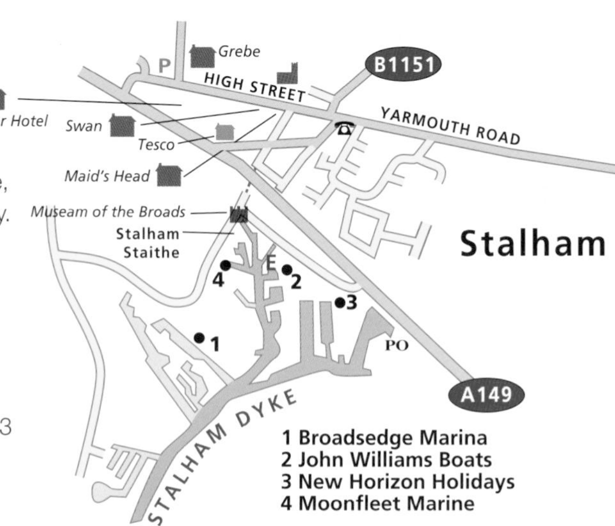

Boatyards and cottages

Broadsedge Marina, Mill Road. Private marina. General boatyard services. Tel: 01692 582881

John Williams Boats, The Staithe. Tel: 01692 580953 E O

Moonfleet Marine, The Staithe. Cruisers, dayboats, houseboats, lodges. Tel: 01692 580288 www.moonfleetmarine.co.uk

♦ O PO ⩚ WC ♦

New Horizon Holidays, The Staithe. Cruisers, café. Tel: 01692 582277 www.newhorizonhols.com

♦ PO ⩚ WC ♦

Pubs

Kingfisher Hotel, High Street. Tel: 01692 581974

The Grebe, High Street. Tel: 01692 580376

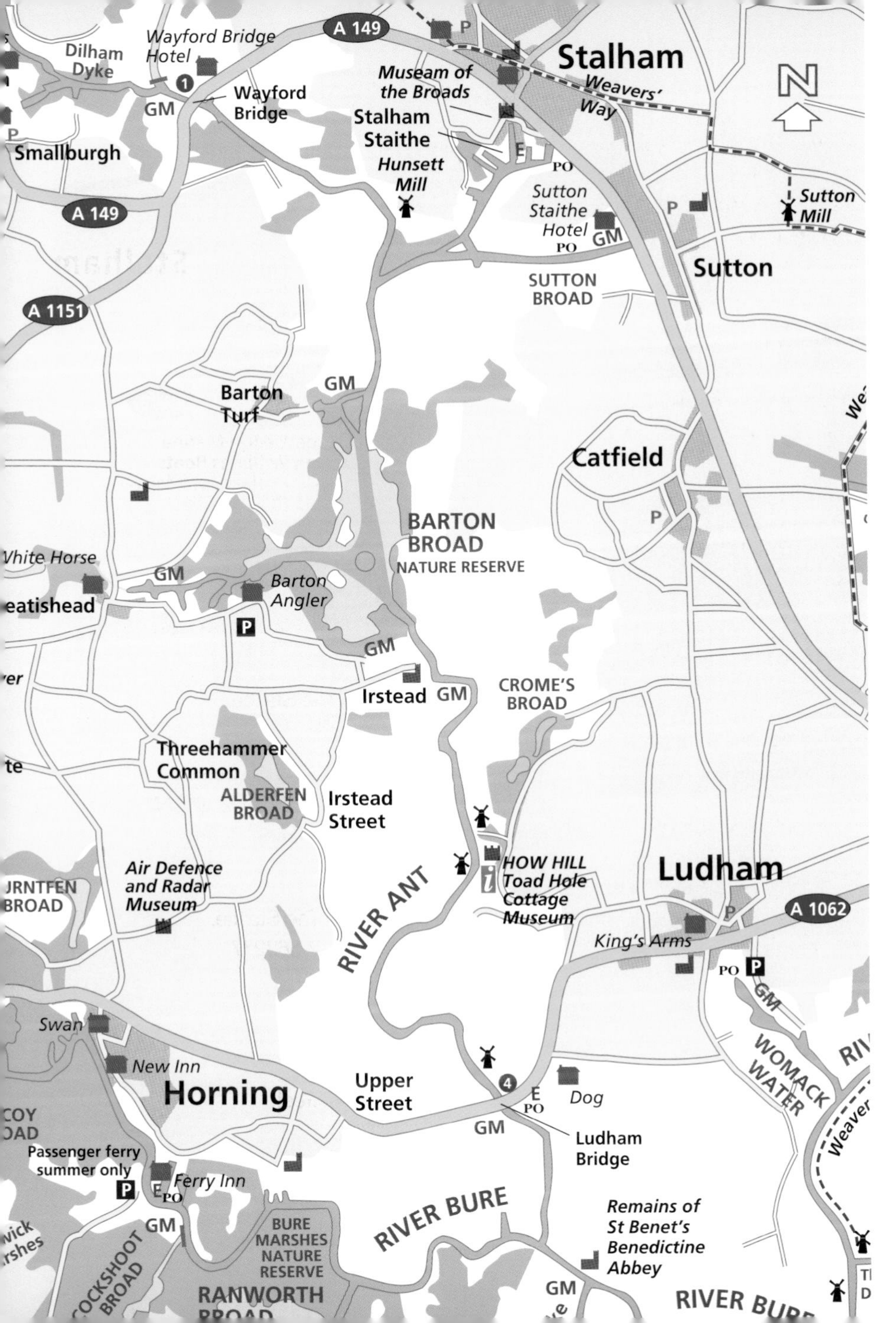

The Maid's Head, High Street.
Tel: 01692 580200

Swan Inn, High Street. Tel: 01692 581492

Wayford Bridge

Travelling north along the Ant, Hunsett Mill, on the right, is now a private home. There are moorings by Wayford Bridge, with a hotel, petrol station with provisions and a farm shop nearby.

Boatyards and cottages

Bank Boats, Staitheside. Dayboats, canoe hire centre, canoe sales.
Tel: 01692 582457

Wayford Marina. Moorings, storage.
Tel: 01692 582555 **PO WC**

Pub *Wayford Bridge Hotel*.
Tel: 01692 582414

Dilham

About 200 metres upstream, the river divides. To the right, the North Walsham and Dilham Canal is only navigable by dinghy. To the left is Dilham Dyke, or Tyler's Cut, leading to Dilham staithe at Brick Kiln Bridge – a short walk from a pub and telephone. The nearest post office, general store and petrol station are at Smallburgh.

Pubs *Cross Keys*, The Street, Dilham.
Tel: 01692 536398
The Crown Inn, North Walsham Road, Smallburgh. Tel: 01692 536314

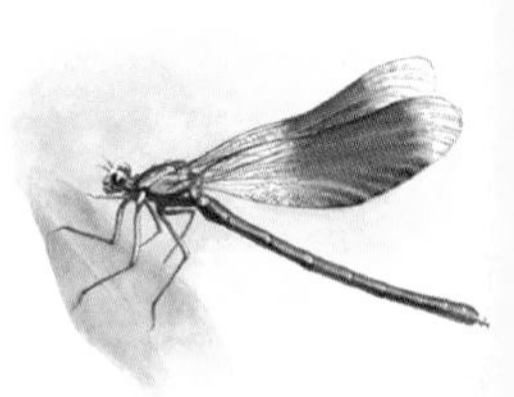

Banded demoiselle

Calopteryx splendens

The male of this common damselfly has a dark metallic blue-green body with a broad dark patch across the wings. The female is a brilliant metallic green. They can be seen between May and August.

River Bure Ant Mouth to Thurne Mouth

Flooded grazing land at St Benet's Abbey

St Benet's Abbey

The ruins of St Benet's Abbey stand beside the River Bure, just past Ant Mouth and opposite the entrance to Fleet Dyke. It can be reached by road from Ludham and Ludham Bridge.

Boats should moor above the ruins to avoid the remains of stonework in the banks. The current is fairly strong. The high and low water tides are about 3½ hours later than at Great Yarmouth Yacht Station.

Founded in the ninth century, on the shore of the estuary to the North Sea, the original abbey was destroyed by Danish invaders in AD 870. About a century later, King Canute founded here what was to become one of the most important monasteries in East Anglia.

In 1536 St Benet's was the only abbey not to be dissolved by Henry XVIII. Instead he appointed the abbot as Bishop of Norwich, with orders to keep a prior and twelve brothers.

Soon after, the monks left and villagers took away the fabric of the monastery to build houses. The mill was built into the ruins of the beautiful arched gateway just over 200 years ago. Today the abbey still has an abbot, prior and ten lay-brothers. On the first Sunday in August each year the Bishop of Norwich, as abbot, holds an open-air service here.

Fleet Dyke and South Walsham Broad

Fleet Dyke, on the other side of the Bure, leads to South Walsham Broad. It is 1 mile *[1.6 km]* long and the rise and fall of the tide is 30 cm *[1 ft]*. There are good moorings at several points along the dyke.

At the end of the dyke is the eastern, or outer part of South Walsham Broad. There is a public quay from which there is a path to the village, 1 mile *[1.6 km]* to the south. The western part of the broad, connected by a narrow strait, is private. Sailing is allowed, but no fishing or mooring. It is shallow near the shore and at the western end.

The route of a circular walk to Upton is shown in the car park at the junction of Broad Lane and Kingfisher Lane.

South Walsham

South Walsham has attractive houses with well tended gardens, a post office and shop, two pubs, and two churches in one churchyard – St Mary's and St Lawrence's – the latter has been restored as a welcoming centre for training and the arts.

The Sacristan's Garden has plants that would have been grown in the fifteenth century – at the time the church was built. The village is on the B1140, 9 miles *[14.5 km]* from Norwich and 3½ miles *[5.6 km]* from Acle.

Fairhaven Water and Woodland Garden is interesting at any time of year, with over 3 miles *[4.8 km]* of easy woodland walks and water trips on South Walsham Inner Broad (see page 27). The garden is organic and a haven for wildlife, with a bird hide.

Boatyard

Russell Marine, Fleet Lane. Cruisers, sailing dinghies, rowboats. Tel: 01603 270262 www.russellmarine.co.uk

PO WC

Pubs *King's Arms*, Panxworth Road. Tel: 01603 270039

The Ship Inn, The Street. Tel: 01603 270049

Thurne Mouth

The Bure, wide and deep, runs through flat meadowland from St Benet's Abbey to Thurne Mouth, with extensive views in all directions. Thurne Church is a noted landmark. The riverbanks are reed and marsh and this is a popular fishing spot. The Bure takes a sharp turn southwards at the point where it meets the River Thurne. There are good moorings here, but the tide runs fast, with a rise and fall of 30 cm *[1 ft]*.

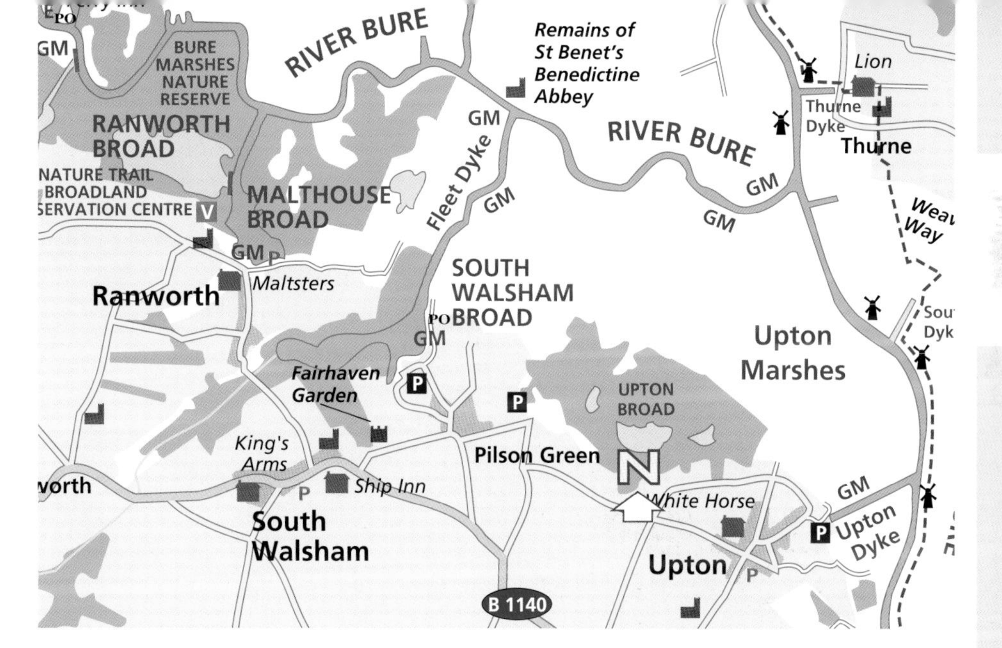

The Sacristan's Garden and St Mary's Church, South Walsham

Ruffe

Gymnocephalus cernua

This small fish has a grey-green back with dark spots, brown sides and a lighter belly. The front part of the dorsal fin is spiny and has black dots between the spines, and the tail also has spots. The ruffe feeds on invertebrates and small fish.

River Thurne Thurne Mouth to Ludham

The Thurne rises near Horsey and Somerton and flows to join the Bure. Near Thurne Mouth, the river courses through flat, almost treeless meadows dotted with windpumps, and the view extends from Acle Bridge to the church at Horning, and to Potter Heigham.

Thurne Mill, at the mouth of Thurne Dyke

Thurne village

Near the mouth on the left is St Benet's Level Mill, and beyond on the right stands *Thurne Dyke Drainage Mill* (see page 28), at the mouth of Thurne Dyke. There are moorings in the dyke and the village has a pub, with restaurant and shop. St Edmund's Church has an embattled tower.

Pub

The Lion Inn, The Street.
Tel: 01692 670796

Ludham

Ludham is a pretty village with thatched cottages and the fourteenth-century St Catherine's Church. The ruins of the abbot's grange of St Benet's Abbey have been incorporated into farm buildings. On the A1062, 4 miles *[6.4 km]* E of Wroxham and 2¼ miles *[3.6 km]* from Potter Heigham, and at the head of Womack Water, Ludham was important in the malt trade. The village has several shops, including a supermarket with post office, a butcher, tearoom, takeaway and pub. *How Hill* is within walking distance (see page 10).

Pub *King's Arms*, High Street.
Tel: 01692 678386

Womack Staithe

By water Ludham is a mile *[1.6 km]* from the Thurne. The dyke is narrow and winding, and the broad is filled with reeds, but there are good moorings at Womack Staithe for a small fee, and full boatyard facilities. The pleasant green has a map of Ludham – a five-minute walk away – and nearby bottle banks, toilets and a well stocked gift shop. A circular walk of about an hour starts beside Hunter's Yard, passes beside Womack Water, near the River Thurne and across Ludham Marshes back to the village.

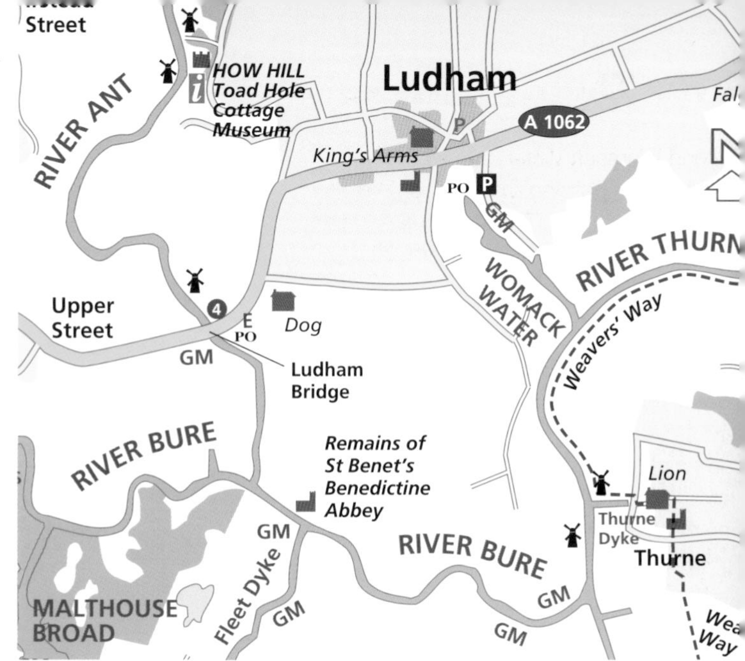

Boatyards

Broadwater Boats, Womack Staithe. Pedaloes. Marine chandler. Free 24-hour breakdown and rescue service.
Tel: 01692 678040

PO

Colin Buttifant, Swallowtail Boatyard, Horsefen Road. Yachts for hire. Tel: 01692 678066 www.swallowtailboats.co.uk

WC

Hunter's Yard, Horsefen Road. Traditional cabin yachts, wooden day-sailers, 2-hour skippered sail, overnight moorings for yachts. Tel: 01692 678263 www.huntersyard.co.uk

WC

River Thurne Potter Heigham to West Somerton

Beyond Womack Water, the River Thurne winds gently, passing moorings at Repps Staithe on the right. Towards Potter Heigham, the banks are lined with riverside chalets.

The low bridge at Potter Heigham

Potter Heigham

The name of this village may be derived from the pottery industry that thrived here in Roman times. 'Heigham', confusingly pronounced as either 'hiyum' or 'heyum', is from the Saxon word for 'town'. The Weavers' Way crosses the striking thirteenth-century arched road bridge.

Potter Heigham is off the A149, Norwich to Great Yarmouth road. Acle can be reached via the B1152, and the A1062 connects with Ludham and Wroxham. There are buses to Great Yarmouth.

A number of shops, including a superstore, cafés and toilets, are close to the river, but the village itself is further north. The Gothic St Nicholas' Church has a thatched roof and round tower with an embattled octagonal belfry stage. The brick font is also octagonal.

There are caravan sites here and at Repps-with-Bastwick, south of the river.

Navigation and moorings

There are good moorings on the right, with access to the village along a path and over the bridge. The public staithe is on the left and there are moorings at the boatyards.

The road bridge is very low and must only be navigated with the help of a pilot. The pick-up point is at Phoenix Fleet boatyard on the right just before the bridge. It is best to arrive two hours before low water. High and low water are about three hours later than at Great Yarmouth Yacht Station.

Broads Information Centre, Bridge Road. Tel: 01692 670779

Helter-skelter cottage at Potter Heigham

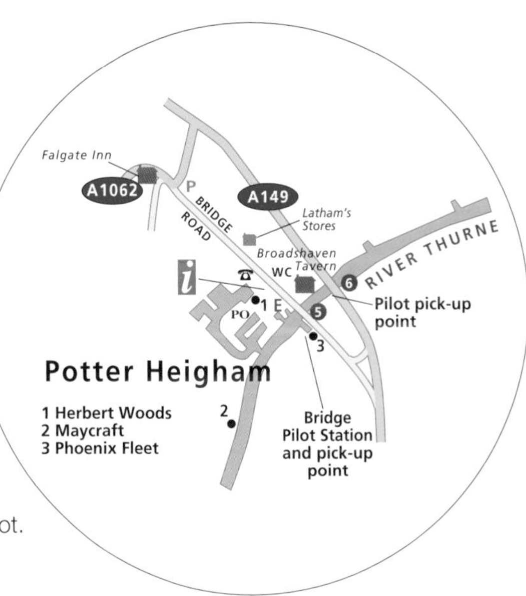

Boatyards and cottages

Herbert Woods, Broadshaven. Motor cruisers, cabin yachts, electric dayboats, passenger craft, apartments, cottages, chandler. Tel: 01692 670711 www.broads.co.uk

E PO WC

Maycraft, North West River Bank. Motor cruisers, dayboats. Tel: 01692 670241 www.maycraft.co.uk PO

Phoenix Fleet, Repps Staithe Boatyard. Electric dayboats. Tel: 01692 670460

Riverside Holidays. Riverside chalets. Tel: 01692 580496

Pubs *Broadshaven Tavern*, Bridge Road. Tel: 01692 670329

Falgate Inn, Ludham Road. Tel: 01692 670003

Milk parsley

Peucedanum palustre

Milk parsley grows amongst the sedge in the reedbeds at the water's edge. It is the food of the rare swallowtail butterfly.

River Thurne

Potter Heigham to West Somerton

The staithe at West Somerton

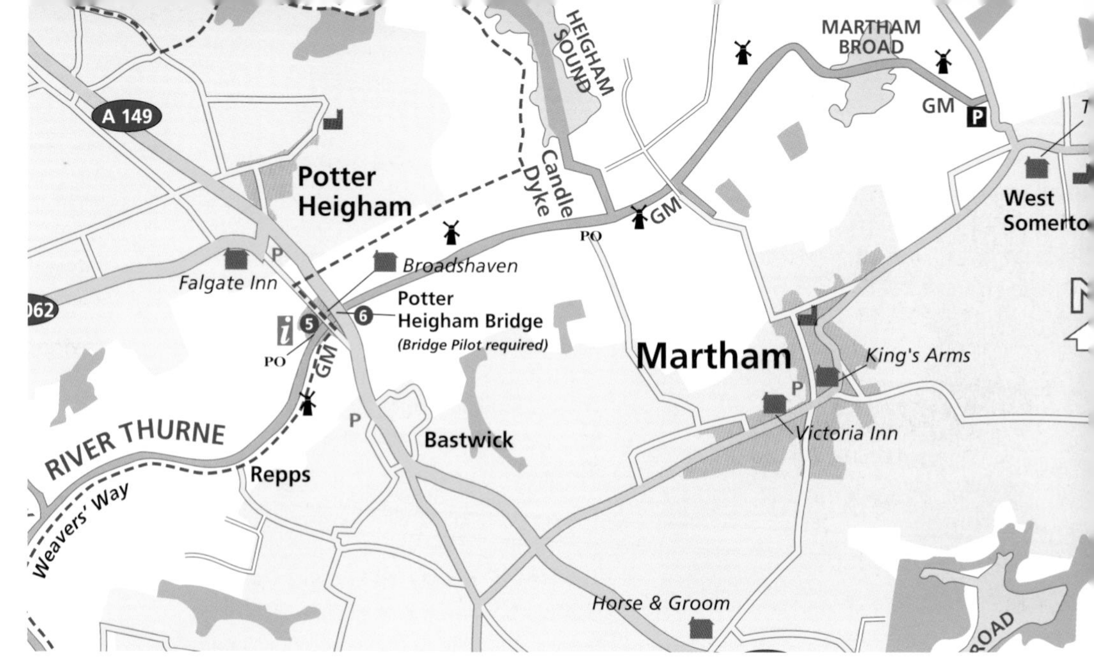

Martham

Further to the west is Candle (Kendal) Dyke, which leads to Heigham Sound (see next section). The stretch of river between the dyke and Martham Broad is popular with anglers. Opposite this dyke are moorings at Martham Boatbuilding and Development Company's yard.

A quarter mile *[400 m]* further on is Martham ferry – private for farm use – and Martham Ferry Boatyard. The village itself lies about a mile *[1.6 km]* from the ferry staithe. It has two supermarkets, and is centred round the Green, which is graced by two duck ponds. The Early Perpendicular church has flint flushwork panels. A circular walk from the village passes the staithe, ferry and Martham Broad.

Great Yarmouth is 9 miles *[14.5 km]* E and Norwich is 18 miles *[29 km]* W. Buses run to the coast and Great Yarmouth.

Boatyard and cottages

Martham Boatbuilding and Development Co., Cess Road. Traditional motor cruisers, cabin yachts, dayboats, houseboats, bungalows. Tel: 01493 740249 www.marthamboats.com

PO WC

Pubs

King's Arms, The Green.
Tel: 01493 740204

The Victoria Inn, Repps Road.
Tel: 01493 740774

Martham or West Somerton Broad

About a mile *[1.6 km]* further on is Martham or West Somerton Broad, a nature reserve managed by the Norfolk Wildlife Trust. Boats should keep to the marked channel. The river eventually merges into the Old Hundred Stream, which centuries ago emptied its water directly into the North Sea though Horsey Gap.

The end of navigation for hire craft is West Somerton, where there are convenient moorings with water, a phone, a pub and St Mary's Church, which has a round tower with an octagonal top and a thatched roof. Robert Hales, the Norfolk giant, is buried in the churchyard. Buses run to Martham, and *Winterton Dunes* (see page 11) and the beach are about 2 miles [3.2 km] E, beyond the modern windfarm.

Pub

The Lion. Tel: 01493 393289

Hickling Broad

Candle Dyke and Heigham Sound

Candle or Kendal Dyke branches north from the River Thurne 1½ miles *[2.4 km]* above Potter Heigham bridge and runs into Heigham Sound, which is shallow and weedy with clearly marked channels. The depth of water is about 1.2 m *[4 ft]*.

Deep Go Dyke, to the left, leads to Whiteslea and *Hickling Broad*, and Meadow Dyke, to the right, connects with *Horsey Mere* (see page 10). There are moorings in Deep Go Dyke and Whiteslea.

Hickling Broad

Hickling has the largest area of open water in the Broads. The centre of a mosaic of reed- and sedgebeds, dykes, grazing meadows, fen and woodland, it supports a rich array of wildlife. The slightly salty water contains rare plants like the holly-leaved naiad. Migrant birds overwinter and breed here, and it is a haven for the bittern and for dragonflies, damselflies and butterflies – in particular the swallowtail.

A footpath of 1½ miles *[2.4 km]* leads from the staithe to the visitor centre, which has a car park. Walking trails, including one suitable for wheelchairs, take visitors through the reedbeds, and the water trail makes use of a traditional reed lighter.

Hickling is 4 miles *[6.4 km]* SE of Stalham and 2½ miles *[4 km]* from Sea Palling. Buses run to Great Yarmouth and Norwich. Sailing and windsurfing clubs are based here. The Pleasure Boat staithe has a cash machine, toilets, a café and gift shop and a phone.

Observation tower at Hickling Broad

Hickling Green, a short walk away, has a post office and general store, a craft shop, pub and repairs garage. *Sutton Mill* (see page 28) is 1½ miles *[2.4 km]* from the staithe.

Navigation and mooring

The channel to the Pleasure Boat is marked by posts – white-tipped to the right and red-tipped to the left. The water is particularly shallow to the left of the entrance to the staithe. Mooring is free for patrons, otherwise there is a fee for mooring, anchoring and angling in the broad, which is renowned for pike fishing in winter.

A channel to the west, where two triangular white markers line up, leads to Catfield Dyke and is suitable for small craft. About halfway, on the left, is Catfield Common Staithe. The public staithe is at the end of the dyke – Catfield is 1¼ miles *[2 km]* away.

Activities

Hickling Broad Sailing Club
www.hicklingbroad.com

Hickling Reserve Visitor Centre.
Tickets for water trail. Tel: 01692 598276
www.norfolkwildlifetrust.org.uk

Hickling Windsurfing Club
www.hicklingbroad.co.uk

Pleasure Boat Café. Cycle hire centre.
Tel: 07747 066606

Eurasian otter

Lutra lutra

These slim brown animals are equally at home on land or in water. Agile swimmers, they feed on fish, including eels, as well as small animals, but usually only spend a short time under the water. Unlike dogs, otters have five toes on each foot. Their holts are made amongst the roots of trees close to rivers, often with underwater entrances. The young pups stay with the mother for a year.

Heigham Sound

Hickling Broad and Horsey Mere

Boatyard

Whispering Reeds Boats, Staithe Road. Cruisers, houseboats, dayboats, sailing dayboats, dinghies, rowboats. Tel: 01692 598314 www.whisperingreeds.net

E PO WC

Pubs

Pleasure Boat Inn. Tel: 01692 598211

Greyhound Inn, The Green.
Tel: 01692 598306

Horsey Windpump and staithe

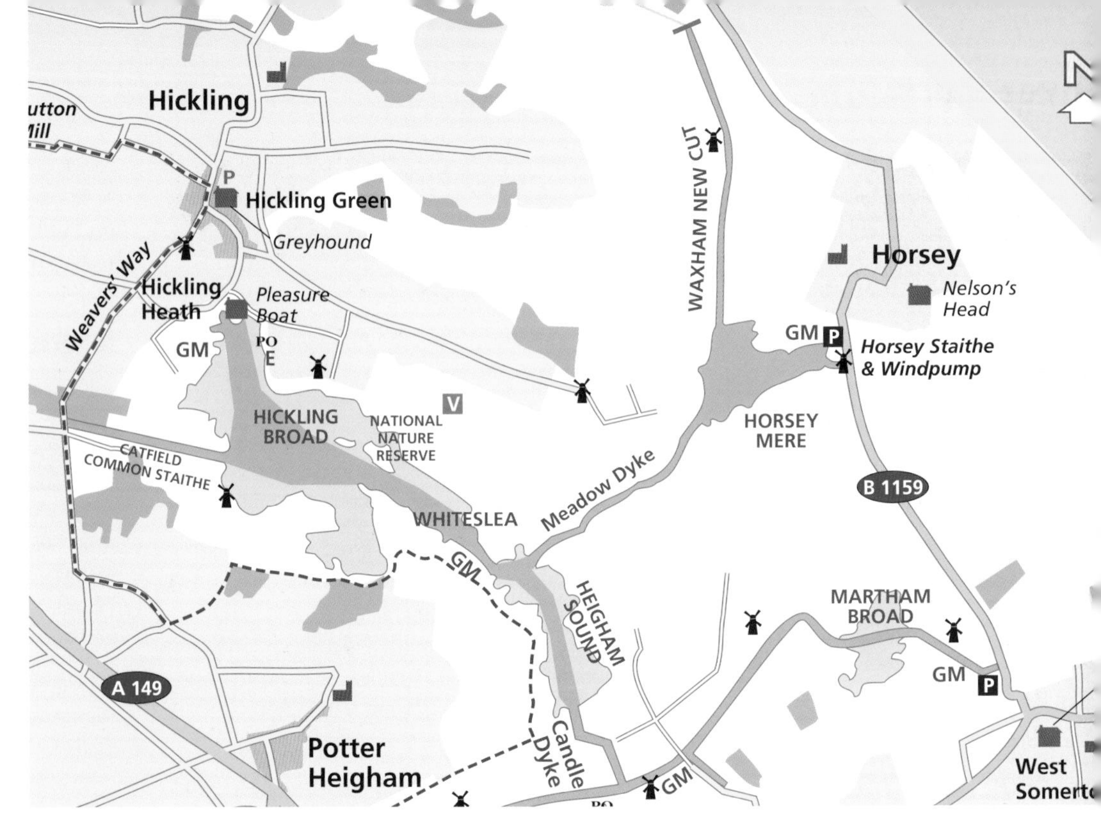

Horsey Mere

Meadow Dyke leads to the right from Heigham Sound to Horsey Mere. The channel is narrow and winding, but the water is fairly deep. When mooring, allow room for passing craft, and keep dinghies under the stern of the boat.

Horsey Mere is a wildfowl sanctuary and is closed to craft during the winter. *Horsey Windpump* (see page 28) is at the far end of the broad. There is a gift shop, toilet block with shower and a pay and display car park for those visiting the mill or taking the circular walk from the staithe along the New Cut and through to Horsey village, about ½ mile *[800 m]* away, where there is a pub and phone. The sea is about 1 mile *[1.6 km]* from Horsey. The beach is steep and sea bathing can be dangerous, with strong currents.

Navigation and moorings

Craft with a deep draught should take a course about 60 yards *[54 m]* N of the island in Horsey Mere. At the east end, near the mill, is a private staithe where boats may moor for a small fee.

Pub

Nelson Head, The Street, Horsey.
Tel: 01493 393378

Waxham New Cut

The entrance to Waxham New Cut is indicated when two white triangular signs on the northern side of Horsey Mere are lined up. It is 1½ miles *[2.4 km]* long and ends at Waxham Bridge. The cut is navigable by boats up to 9 metres *[30 ft]* in length.

Upton staithe

Travelling south from Thurne Mouth, there are moorings on the left bank. The tidal range here is about 30 cm *[1 ft]*. High and low tides are about 3½ hours after Great Yarmouth Yacht Station. Oby Dyke on the left is private. Tall Mill on the right is almost opposite the entrance to South Oby Dyke, also private. Oby Mill, or Wiseman's Mill, stands on the left bank.

Upton Dyke and village

Just over 1½ miles *[2.4 km]* below Thurne Mouth and 1¼ miles *[2 km]* above Acle Bridge is the entrance to Upton Dyke. This runs west to a staithe near Upton village and provides good moorings, but is quite narrow. There is a small slipway, car park with rubbish bins and a boatyard. The route of a circular walk along the Bure from Upton Dyke to South Walsham Broad is given on a board in the car park.

The landlocked Upton Broad

Upton has a pub and post office with some provisions, and St Margaret's, a surprisingly large church in the Perpendicular style. A footpath from The Green leads through fields to Acle.

Boatyard

Eastwood Whelpton, Upton Dyke.
Yacht station. Tel: 01493 450430
WC 💧

Pub

White Horse. Tel: 01493 750696

Upton Fen

Upton Broad, about ½ mile *[800 m]* NW of the dyke, is spring fed and not accessible by water, but the adjoining *Upton Fen* is a nature reserve with waymarked trails, and is known for its dragonflies (see page 10). There is a small car park off Low Road South Walsham. Stout shoes or boots are recommended.

Acle Bridge

This, the only bridge over the Bure between Wroxham and Great Yarmouth, carries the A1064 and the Weavers' Way long-distance path. A car park with toilets and rubbish compound lies behind the well-stocked Bridge Stores, and there is a coffee shop beside the pub and a telephone near the boatyard entrance.

Acle is about a mile *[1.6 km]* S of the bridge. Buses run to Great Yarmouth and Norwich. *Thrigby Hall Wildlife Gardens* are about 3½ miles *[5.6 km]* away, on the Stokesby to Filby road (see page 25).

Bowline

This knot makes a strong loop at the end of a rope and can also be used to join two ropes.

River Bure

Thurne Mouth to Stracey Arms

Navigation and moorings

There are moorings either side of the bridge and three boatyards. The tide runs fast, with a rise and fall of between 38 and 53 cm *[1 ft 3 in–1ft 9 in]*. High and low water are about three hours after Great Yarmouth Yacht Station. The best time for power craft to leave for Great Yarmouth is five hours after high water.

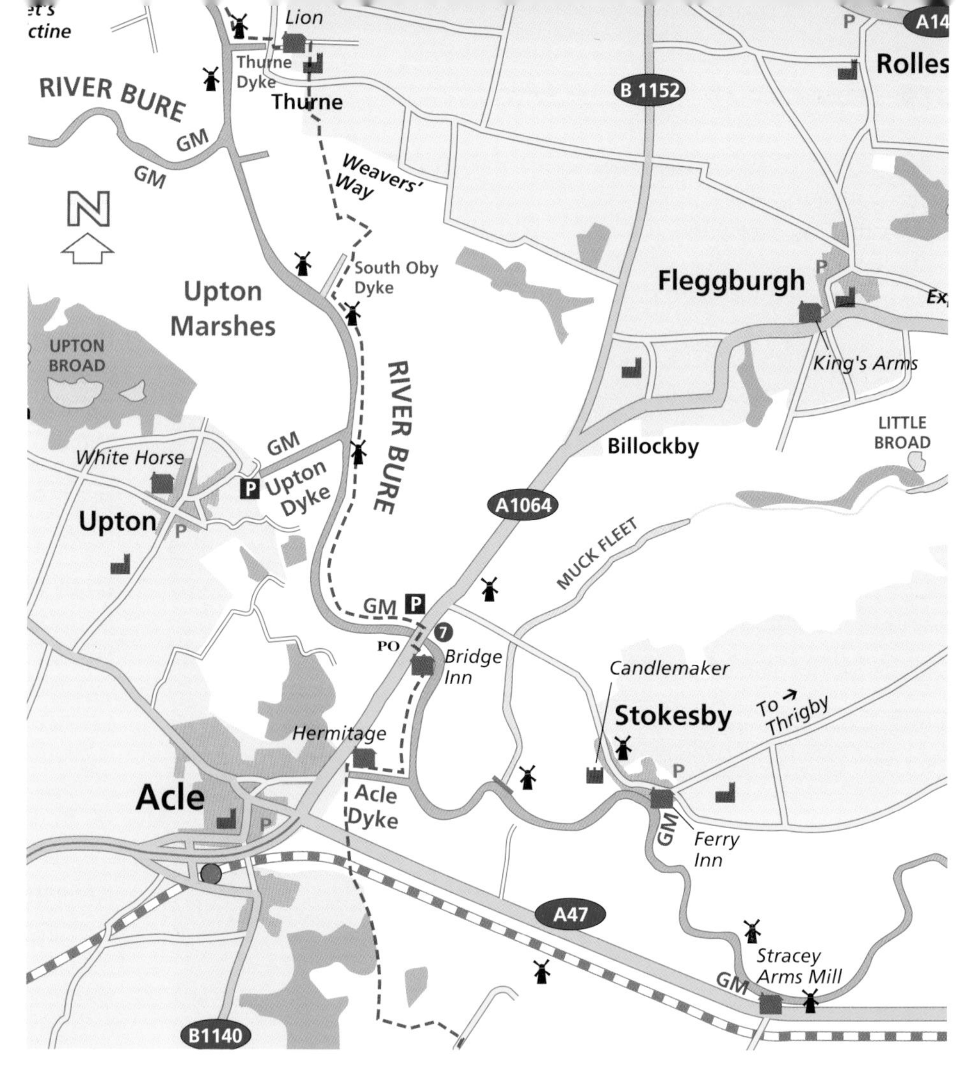

The Three Rivers Race from Acle Bridge

Boatyards

Bridgecraft. Motor cruisers, dayboats. Tel: 0870 4059479 www.hoseasons.co.uk

PO

Horizon Craft. Motor cruisers. Tel: 01493 582277 www.newhorizonhols.com

PO WC

Pub

The Bridge Inn. Tel: 01493 750288

Acle Dyke

The dyke is narrow, but there is a public staithe and a pub nearby. The centre of Acle is a short walk away.

Acle

This small market town has a long history. Acle was granted a market during the thirteenth century and still holds a produce market and furniture auction on Thursdays. The town has various other facilities, including two supermarkets, three hotels, a health centre and a vet.

St Edmund's Church has a round Saxon tower with an octagonal top added in the thirteenth century and a thatched roof. The origins of the nave are thought to be Norman, and a charcoal inscription asks for protection for the village from the Black Death.

Acle is just off the A47, 11½ miles *[18 km]* from Norwich and 8½ miles *[13.5 km]* from Great Yarmouth. There are regular train and bus services from both.

Pubs *King's Head*, The Street.
Tel: 01493 750204
Hermitage Restaurant and Pub, Old Road. Tel: 01493 750310

The Trinity Broads

Muck Fleet, on the northern side of the Bure, is not navigable. It is the outlet of Ormesby, Rollesby and Filby Broads, which together are known as the Trinity Broads. Rollesby Broad lies between the A149 and B1064, with Ormesby Broad to

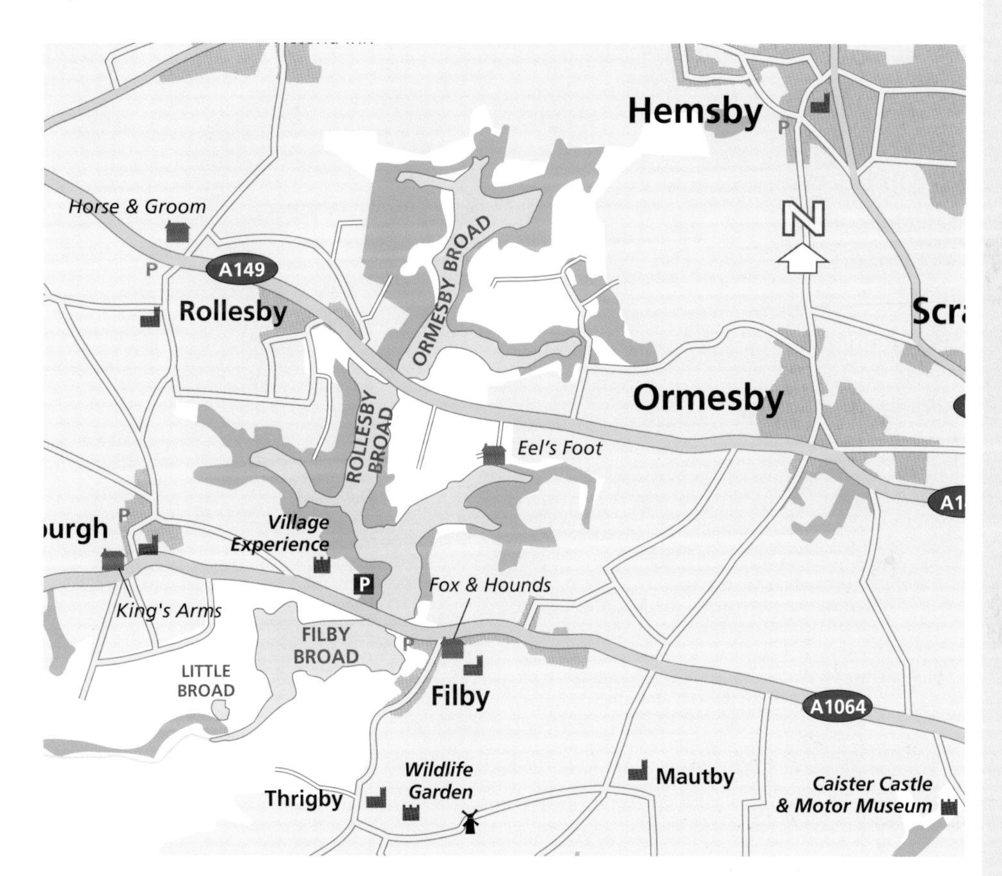

the north and Filby Broad to the south. Only a few sailing and angling craft are allowed on these waters. Dinghies can be hired at Ormesby, Rollesby and Filby, and the Eel's Foot Inn has a wheelyboat. A car park at Filby Broad leads to a boardwalk and an accessible bird hide.

Pubs
Eel's Foot Inn, Ormesby.
Tel: 01493 730342
Fox and Hounds, Filby.
Tel: 01493 369255

Stokesby

Stokesby is a tranquil village at what was a crossing point over the Bure until the early twentieth century. Off the A1064, it is 2 miles *[3.2 km]* from Acle Bridge by river and 9 miles *[14.5 km]* from Great Yarmouth. There is a post office, general store and tearooms, candle craft centre

Comma
Polygonium c-album

This butterfly has golden-brown black-spotted wings with jagged edges. Its name comes from a 'c'-shaped white mark on the underside of each hind wing. The caterpillars, which feed on nettle plants, are dark and spiny and have a broad white stripe for half their length. The butterflies can be seen in July and August.

River Bure Thurne Mouth to Stracey Arms

Cottage at Stokesby

(see page 25) and pub. The fourteenth-century church of St Andrew stands northeast of the village.

Buses run regularly to Acle and to Great Yarmouth and bikes can be hired. *Thrigby Hall Wildlife Gardens* are only 2½ miles *[4 km]* away (see page 25) and it is about 5½ miles *[9 km]* to *Caister Castle Car Collection* (see page 29). The route of a circular walk beside Muck Fleet and the Bure is shown on a board close to the moorings.

Navigation and moorings

There are good moorings by the Ferry Inn and rubbish bins nearby. The tide has a rise and fall of 61 cm *[2 ft]*, and the ebb and flow is fast. High and low tide are about 2 hours 40 minutes after Great Yarmouth Yacht Station. The best time for powered craft to leave for Great Yarmouth is five hours after high water.

Cycle hire

Riverside Tea Rooms and Stores.
Tel: 01493 750470

Pub *Ferry Inn*. Tel: 01493 751096

Stracey Arms Mill, Tunstall

The Stracey Arms Mill, shop and tearooms are close to the river. Next door is an American diner, in what used to be a pub named after Lady Stracey. This is the only stop on the Acle Straight, part of the A47, 6 miles *[9.5 km]* from Great Yarmouth, 2½ miles *[4 km]* from Acle, and 13¾ miles *[22 km]* from Norwich.

Navigation and moorings

There is a good quay with deep water at this last good mooring place above Great Yarmouth, which is 8 miles *[13 km]* away by water. The tide flows fast and the rise and fall is about 61 cm *[2 ft]*. High and low water are about 2½ hours later than at Great Yarmouth Yacht Station. It takes about 1½ hours to reach the yacht station, so the best time for powered craft to leave is five hours after high water.

Holly blue butterfly

Stracey Arms Mill

The Bure is winding in its lower reaches, with many shoals of shelving mud, and care is needed to keep well within the channel, particularly at low water. It is not advisable to moor, as the rise and fall of the tide is between 91 cm and 1.2 m *[3–4 ft]*. In emergencies boats should tie up at any one of the houses. There are footpaths from those on the right bank to the A47.

Great Yarmouth

Great Yarmouth is a large seaside resort with all kinds of facilities (see page 20). Regular rail services run to Norwich, via Reedham or Acle, connecting with London, Cambridge and the north, and national coach services stop here. Buses run to Norwich, Lowestoft and many local villages.

Navigation and moorings

The Bure meets the River Yare close to the sea and ebb tides are particularly strong, so the best time to arrive at Great Yarmouth is at slack water, about 1½ hours after low water. This also gives maximum headroom under the bridges. Masts and cockpit canopies must be lowered.

There are free daytime moorings at Marina Keys, which has a riverside café and pub, and adjoins Bure Park. It is also handy for Great Yarmouth Racecourse and for the stadium, where greyhound racing and stock-car racing take place regularly.

Craft can also moor free at Great Yarmouth Yacht Station during the day. It may be necessary to moor abreast at busy times. It is important to come alongside the quay against the tidal flow. This can be tricky at ebb tide in a sailing craft without an auxiliary motor, which will need to make use of a mud weight to turn and then tack backwards. The average rise and fall of the tide is 1.4 m *[4 ft 6 in]*.

Great Yarmouth Yacht Station

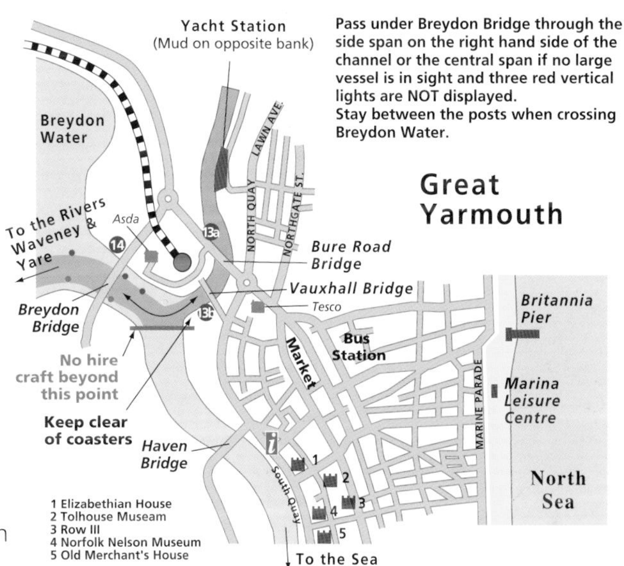

Help is available from Broads Authority quay rangers at the yacht station. Give the name of the boat, the exact location and the type of help needed.

The moorings near the road bridge are for yachts to lower or raise their masts.

Great Yarmouth Yacht Station, Lawn Avenue. Washing facilities. Filling station nearby. Tel: 01493 842794

WC

Marina Keys, Caister Road. Launderette. Tel: 01493 842600

PO WC

Navigating the bridges

The Bure Road Bridge and Vauxhall Bridge are both low and should be

Water vole

Arvicola terrestris

Water voles are vegetarians. They live in burrows in the riverbank, with entrances at the waterline and underwater that lead up to dry nest chambers. Because their tails are long, they are sometimes known as water rats.

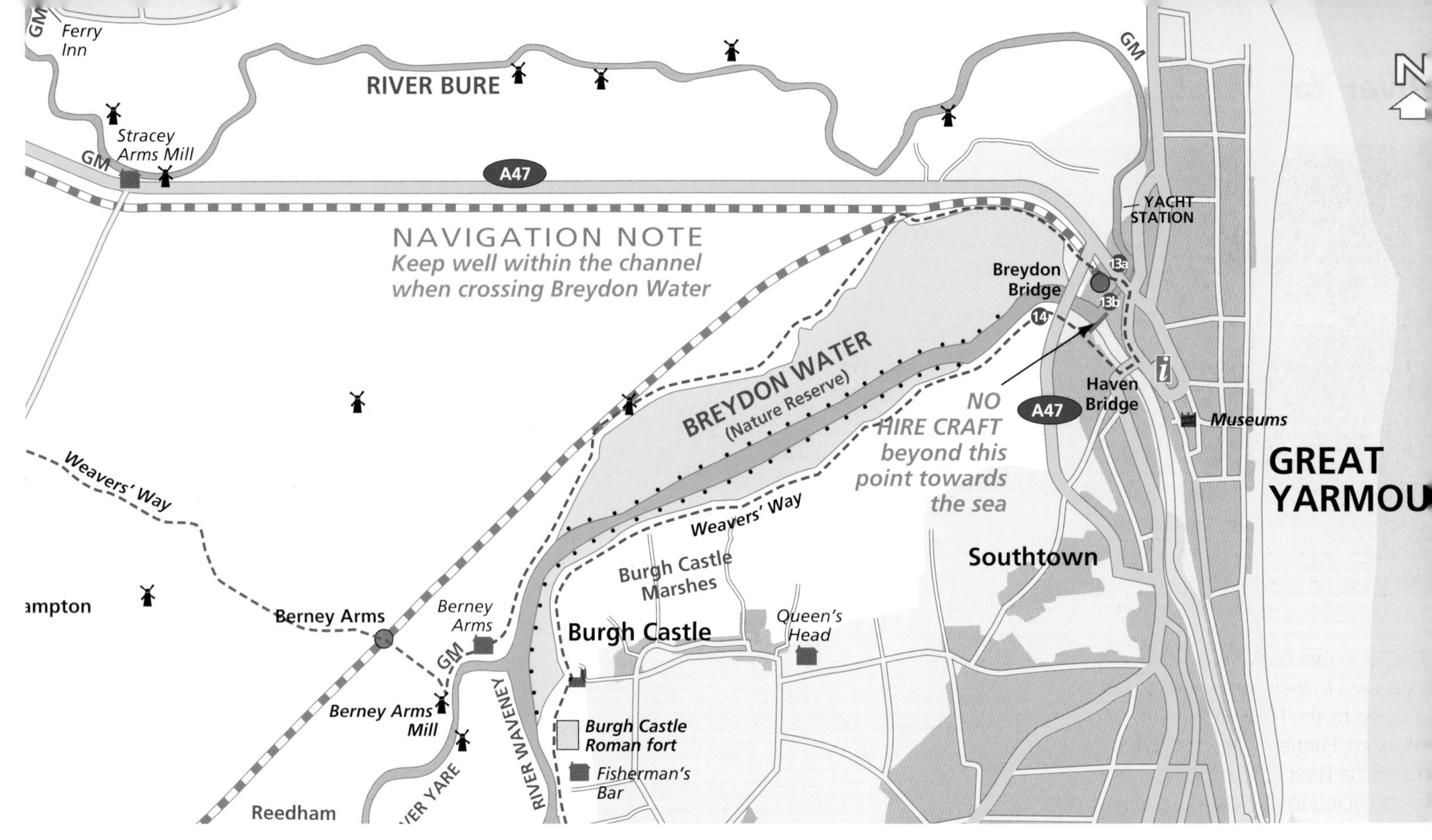

approached with care. Boat height should be checked before passing under both bridges below the red arrows. Stop if three vertical red lights are lit on the bridge.

No hire craft are allowed into the harbour, so craft need to keep right towards Breydon Bridge, watching out for coasters mooring at the quay on the left. A right turn can be made after the yellow post.

Breydon Bridge has three navigation spans. The side spans have air draft of 4.5 m *[14 ft 9 in]* and the main lifting span 4 m *[13 ft 1 in]* at mean high water spring tides. Craft should use the right-hand span through the channel marked by red triangles. Three red stoplights are fixed on either side of the main navigation span and vessels should not approach the main channel when the lights are showing. These do not affect navigation under the side spans, but indicate that commercial vessels may be manoeuvring. Beyond the bridge is Breydon Water, leading to the rivers Waveney and Yare.

Breydon Bridge

Berney Arms Windmill and Breydon Water

The River Yare rises west of Norwich and meanders to the south of the city, where it is joined by the River Tas and then by the Wensum. Further to the east the Yare meets the River Chet near Reedham and is connected to the River Waveney by the New Cut. It flows through Breydon Water and into the North Sea at Great Yarmouth.

Breydon Water

The remains of a huge estuary that used to extend to Beccles and Norwich, *Breydon Water* teems with waterfowl and seabirds (see page 9). It has been silting up for centuries, but a wide deep channel is maintained across the 4 miles *[6.4 km]* of Breydon and there is no danger of running aground if craft stay between the marked stakes.

Navigation and moorings

A navigation ranger patrols Breydon Water. If in doubt about crossing, contact your boatyard or river control. Keep the green or black stakes to the right and red stakes to the left when crossing from Yarmouth and vice versa in the other direction. (Be prepared for the bridges by reading the information opposite.)

It is high and low water at the western end one hour later than at Great Yarmouth Yacht Station, and the tide runs fast. The Yare forks to the west and the Waveney to the south. There are no safe moorings on Breydon – the nearest are at Berney Arms and Burgh Castle.

River control. Tel: 01692 678459

Berney Arms

This most remote Broadland pub is only accessible by water, on foot or by train. *Berney Arms Windmill* is a distinctive landmark (see page 28). *Berney Marshes* (see page 9) are part of Halvergate grazing marshes. Water levels are controlled to produce shallow flooding in the winter and spring, attracting wildfowl and waders and benefiting other marshland wildlife. In spring the damp grassland is ideal for nesting species.

There are safe moorings between the inn and mill. The next are at Reedham, although there is emergency mooring on the north bank near Seven Mile House, where three mills can be seen.

Pub

Berney Arms Inn. Tel: 01493 700303

Ruff

Philomachus pugnax

In winter both male and female are grey-brown and mottled, with white beneath, but between April and July the male has an impressive ruff around its neck, which may be black, white, brown or red and is extended for display. Ruff can be seen in winter at several sites, including Berney Marshes.

River Waveney Burgh Castle to Somerleyton

The River Waveney at Burgh Castle

The River Waveney rises to the west of Bungay and in the past carried ships to that town. The limit of navigation for Broads visitors is Geldeston Lock, at Shipmeadow, 3 miles *[4.8 km]* west of Beccles. The river flows northeast for 22 miles *[35 km]* until it merges with the Yare at Breydon Water.

The New Cut at St Olaves is a canal that connects with the Yare, shortening the distance to Norwich by water. A dyke leads to Oulton Broad and through a lock, the end of navigation for hire craft, to Lake Lothing and so to the North Sea at Lowestoft. The river is tidal to Geldeston Lock.

Burgh Castle

Three massive walls and parts of the towers of the Roman fort of Gariannonum still remain at Burgh Castle, close to Breydon Water. Built at the end of the third century at the edge of the huge estuary, the fort was part of a chain of fortifications to guard the east coast. In the seventh century the Irish missionary St Fursey founded a monastery on the site, which was later turned back into a castle by the Normans.

The village of Burgh Castle is off the A143, near Great Yarmouth and has two pubs. There are several campsites in the area.

The Bell Inn, St Olaves

Navigation and moorings

Craft should not moor close to the castle as there is little depth, even at high water, and it is easy to become stranded. There are free moorings for patrons at the Fisherman's Bar and a footpath from here leads to the castle. Burgh Castle Yacht Station offers moorings and boatyard services. There are free moorings just upstream. Average tidal rise and fall is from 1.15 to 1.25 m *[3 ft 9 in–4 ft 1 in]*.

Boatyard and marina

Burgh Castle Marina, Butt Lane. Quiet family campsite with swimming pool, laundry facilities, disability access. Tel: 01493 780331 www.burghcastlemarina.co.uk

Goodchild Marine Services, Burgh Castle Yacht Station, Butt Lane. Dayboat, chandlery, storage, towing. Tel: 01493 782301 www.goodchild-marine.co.uk

Pubs

Fisherman's Bar, Burgh Castle Marina. Tel: 01493 780729

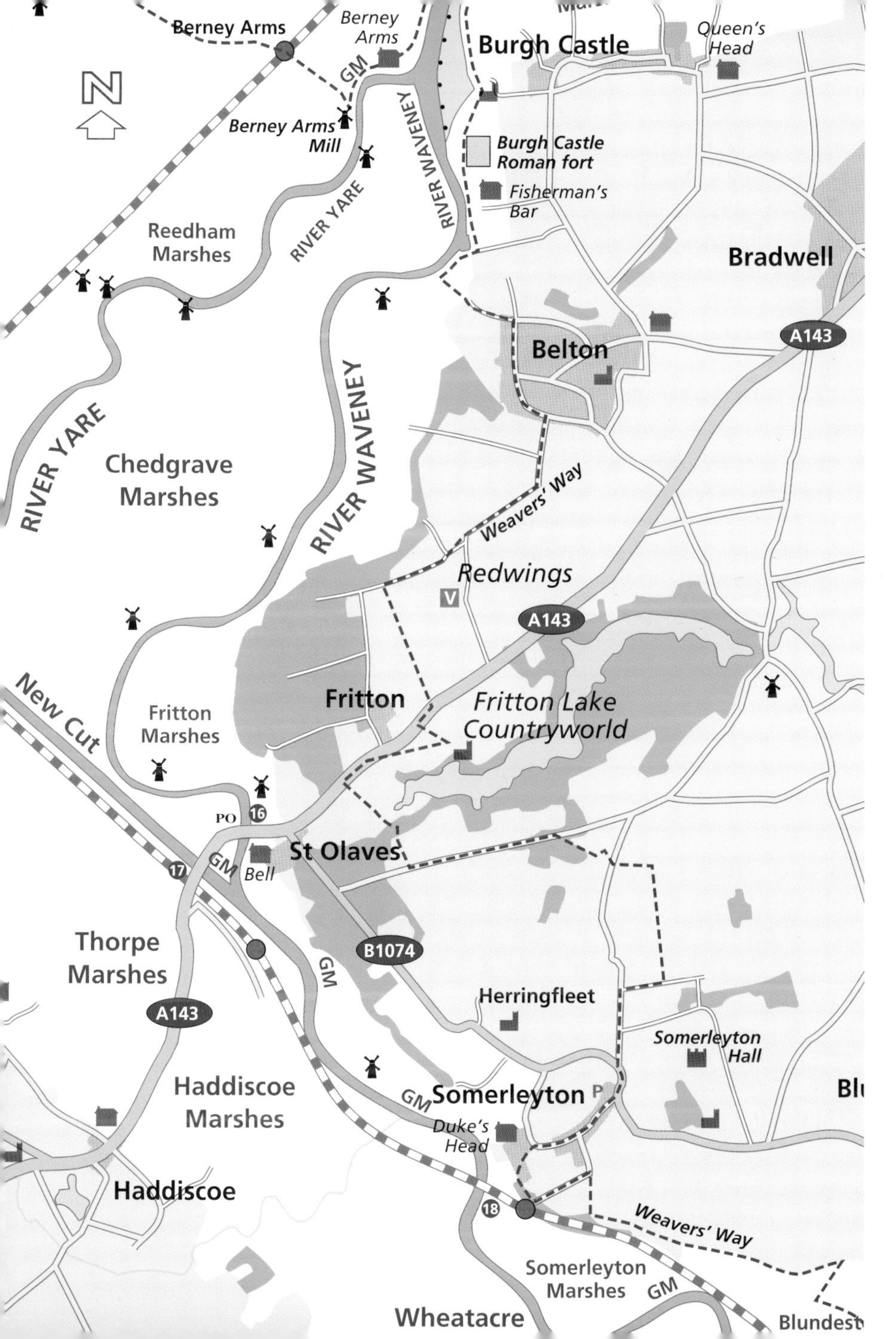

Queen's Head, High Road.
Tel: 01493 780363

St Olaves

St Olave's Windpump (see page 28) is a small boarded trestle mill on the left. It can be reached by a footpath from the village. Beside it is Blocka Run, which connects with Fritton Lake, but is not navigable. There are free moorings before the mill.

The village of St Olaves is on the A143 between Great Yarmouth and Beccles, near the junction with the New Cut. Both the river and the New Cut are crossed by road bridges. St Olaves has a pub, provisions shop and filling station with phone close by. The ruins of the Augustinian Priory of St Olaves and St Mary, founded about 1216, have been excavated and partly restored and can be visited. The priory's bakehouse and brewery form part of an adjoining farm. A column of the priory's refectory stands on a Roman millstone.

There is a rail station at Haddiscoe, on the other side of the New Cut about 1¼ miles *[2 km]* away. The New Cut itself carries craft to Reedham on the River Yare.

Navigation and moorings

High and low water are about 1½ hours after Great Yarmouth Yacht Station. The tide runs fast and there is a rise and fall of 76 to 91 cm *[2 ft 6 in–3 ft]*. It is best to moor into the current. The headroom of the bridge is 2.5 m *[8 ft 4 in]*.

Mink

Mustela vison

The mink was brought to England in the 1920s and farmed to provide fur for then-fashionable coats. Animals escaped and thrived in the wild, feeding on small mammals, waterfowl, birds and fish. The body of a mink is about 61 cm *[2 ft]* long and the tail can be another 25 cm *[10 in]*. The females produce five or six young, known as kittens.

River Waveney Burgh Castle to Somerleyton

The Bell Inn originally had a bell for summoning the ferryman before a bridge was built. It has moorings for patrons and there are moorings at boatyards.

Boatyards

Alpha Craft. Cruisers. Tel: 01603 713265
www.norfolkbroadsboatingholidays.com

PO WC

Castle Craft, Reeds Lane. Cruisers, dayboats, cranage. Tel: 01493 488675

PO

Pub

Bell Inn, Beccles Road. Tel: 01493 488249

Fritton Lake, Somerleyton

Fritton

The village of Fritton is about 1 mile *[1.6 km]* NE of St Olaves, along the A143. This is the location of *Fritton Lake, Somerleyton* (see page 27), which has a variety of activities for people of all ages, both on the lake and in the grounds. The lake is surrounded by trees and parkland and is famous for its decoys, used in the past for catching wildfowl.

St Edmund's Church, in the village, has an apsidal chancel of late Saxon or early Norman date and wall paintings of St John and St Christopher.

Redwings Horse Sanctuary (see page 25) is at nearby Caldecott Hall.

Somerleyton

Herringfleet Mill (see page 28) is between St Olaves and Somerleyton, with access from the B1074.

St Margaret's Church at Herringfleet is early Norman, of flint with stone facings, and has ancient stained glass and a round tower.

Somerleyton itself was inhabited 3,000 years ago, according to the evidence of late bronze age implements found near the Rectory. This pretty estate village is just off the B1074, close to *Somerleyton Hall* (see page 26), an early Victorian country mansion with extensive gardens and a yew hedge maze. St Mary's Church has a sixteenth-century screen with fifteen painted panels.

Somerleyton post office

There is a provisions shop, tearoom and post office, pub and rail station with services to Lowestoft and Norwich, and the line crosses the river at this point.

Navigation and moorings

The tide is apt to run strongly under the bridge, with a rise and fall of 91 cm *[3 ft]*. High and low water are about 2½ hours later than at Great Yarmouth Yacht Station. Unless two red flags are displayed, the bridge will be swung when rail traffic permits. There is headroom at average high water of 2.4 m *[8 ft]*. Good moorings can be found north of the bridge on the east bank.

Pub *Duke's Head*, Slugs Lane.
Tel: 01502 730281

Somerleyton to Oulton Dyke

The banks are reedy, so mooring is not recommended, but there is an emergency mooring on the left opposite Black Mill and another just before Oulton Dyke, with a footpath to Oulton Broad.

Oulton Broad

Oulton Dyke

This dyke connects the Waveney and Oulton Broad. There are few good moorings. The rise and fall of tide is 61 cm *[2 ft]*. High water is about the same as Oulton Broad. The dyke is a noted fishing ground.

Yachts racing at Oulton Broad

Oulton Broad

One of the finest inland yachting lakes in Britain, Oulton Broad is also a popular centre for windsurfing and fishing, and powerboat race meetings have been held here for over 75 years. Racing takes place on Thursday evenings and bank holidays in summer and can be watched from Nicholas Everitt Park. The yacht club is based at the eastern end of the broad, just south of the yacht station.

There is a range of facilities and shops in Oulton Broad itself, and next-door *Lowestoft* (see page 23) is the leading Suffolk seaside resort.

Trains run to Lowestoft and London, via Ipswich, from South Station, and a service between Norwich and Lowestoft operates from North Station. Buses connect Lowestoft with Norwich, Great Yarmouth and London.

Lowestoft and Oulton Broad Motor Boat Club.
www.lobmbc.co.uk

Waveney and Oulton Broad Yacht Club.
www.saileast.co.uk/wobyc

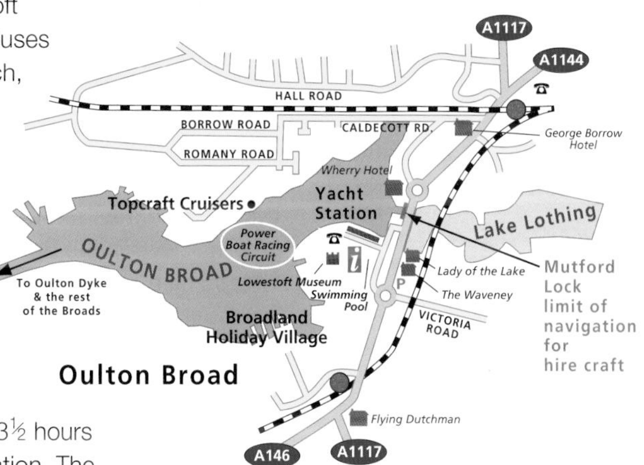

Navigation and moorings

High and low water are about 3½ hours after Great Yarmouth Yacht Station. The rise and fall is about 61 cm *[2 ft]*. The yacht station has wide berths for yachts and cruisers, and there are moorings at Broadland Holiday Village and Topcraft Cruisers.

Rowing ashore at Oulton Broad

Boatyards

Broadland Holiday Village, Marsh Road. Bungalows, swimming pool, launderette, Tel: 01502 573033
www.broadlandvillage.co.uk
PO WC

Oulton Broad Day Boats, Yacht Station. Dayboats, rowboats. Tel: 01502 589556

Oulton Broad Yacht Station, The Boulevard. Bathrooms, drying rooms, electric points on pontoon. Tel: 01502 574946 **WC**

Topcraft Cruisers, Caldecott Road. Cruisers. Tel: 0870 4059479 **PO**

Waveney River Tours, Mutford Lock, Bridge Road. Tel: 01502 574903

Pubs

Commodore, Commodore Road. Tel: 01502 565955

Flying Dutchman, Beccles Road. Tel: 01502 561391

Lady of the Lake, Bridge Road. Tel: 01502 574740

Waveney, Bridge Road. Tel: 01502 573940

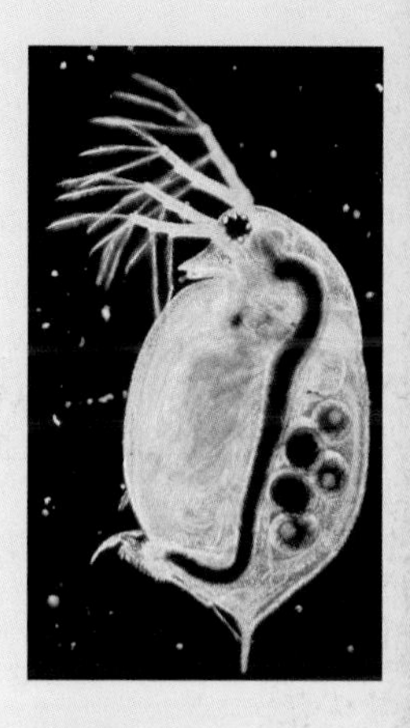

Water flea
Daphnia

The tiny water flea is part of the freshwater plankton. It is important in keeping the water clear so that other water creatures and plants can survive. *Daphnia* feed on algae, microscopic animals and debris, and have been used in the management of Barton Broad to improve the water quality. Fish-free areas have been created to allow the *Daphnia* to thrive.

River Waveney Oulton Dyke to Beccles

Burgh St Peter

Good moorings can be found at the Waveney River Centre, Burgh St Peter, with a pub, restaurant, shop, campsite, children's play area, pool and gym. There are also splendid views over the Waveney valley. The village itself is 1¾ miles *[2.8 km]* from the quay. The tower of St Mary's Church is built in a series of steps, each of the four sections diminishing as they ascend.

Boatyard

Waveney River Centre, Burgh St Peter Staithe. Leisure centre, dayboats, electric hook-ups, oil. Tel: 01502 677343 www.waveneyrivercentre.co.uk

Burgh St Peter to Beccles

The river winds through marshes with stretches of trees. There are good moorings in places, but some bays are shallow and there is shelving. Yacht racing takes place in the stretch just before Beccles at the weekends.

A wherry on the Waveney at Beccles

Beccles

Beccles is a historic market town with several good pubs, large supermarkets, specialist shops, restaurants, cafés, banks and building societies and an outdoor heated swimming pool. The stretch of the river through the town makes one of the loveliest views in the Broads, and angling is good here.

The fourteenth-century St Michael's Church has a detached bell-tower, which is 28 m *[92 ft]* high. Horatio Nelson's parents, the Reverend Edward Nelson and Catherine Suckling, were married here in 1749. The Beccles Museum, with displays about local trades, including clockmaking, is on Ballygate.

A trip on Liana *at Beccles*

Trains run to London, Ipswich and Lowestoft. Buses connect with Lowestoft and Great Yarmouth. River trips on the electric-powered *Liana* can be booked at the information centre.

Broads Information Centre, The Quay, Fen Lane. Tel: 01502 713196

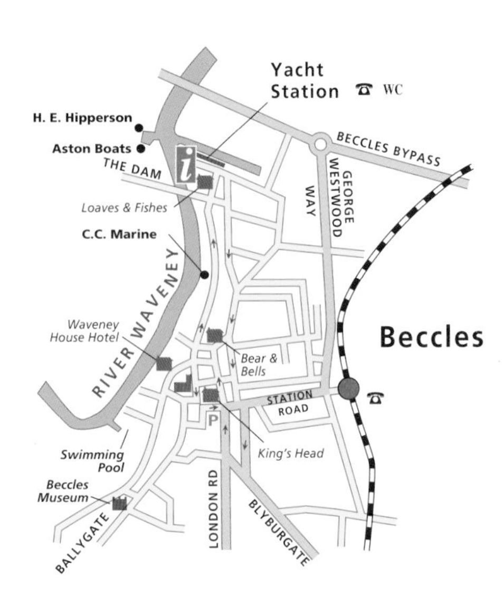

Navigation and moorings

There are two fixed road bridges. Care is needed at high water. High and low water are about three hours later than at Great Yarmouth Yacht Station. There is an average rise and fall of tide of 61 to 76 cm *[2 ft–2 ft 6 in]* and in spring tides sometimes 1.06 m *[3 ft 6 in]*.

There are good stern-on moorings at the yacht station, which is in the Cut at the northern end of Beccles, and moorings at the boatyards. Further upstream, there is a small pontoon mooring at the public swimming pool.

Boatyards

Aston Boats, Bridge Wharf. Cruisers, rowboats, oil. Tel: 01502 713960 www.astonboats.com

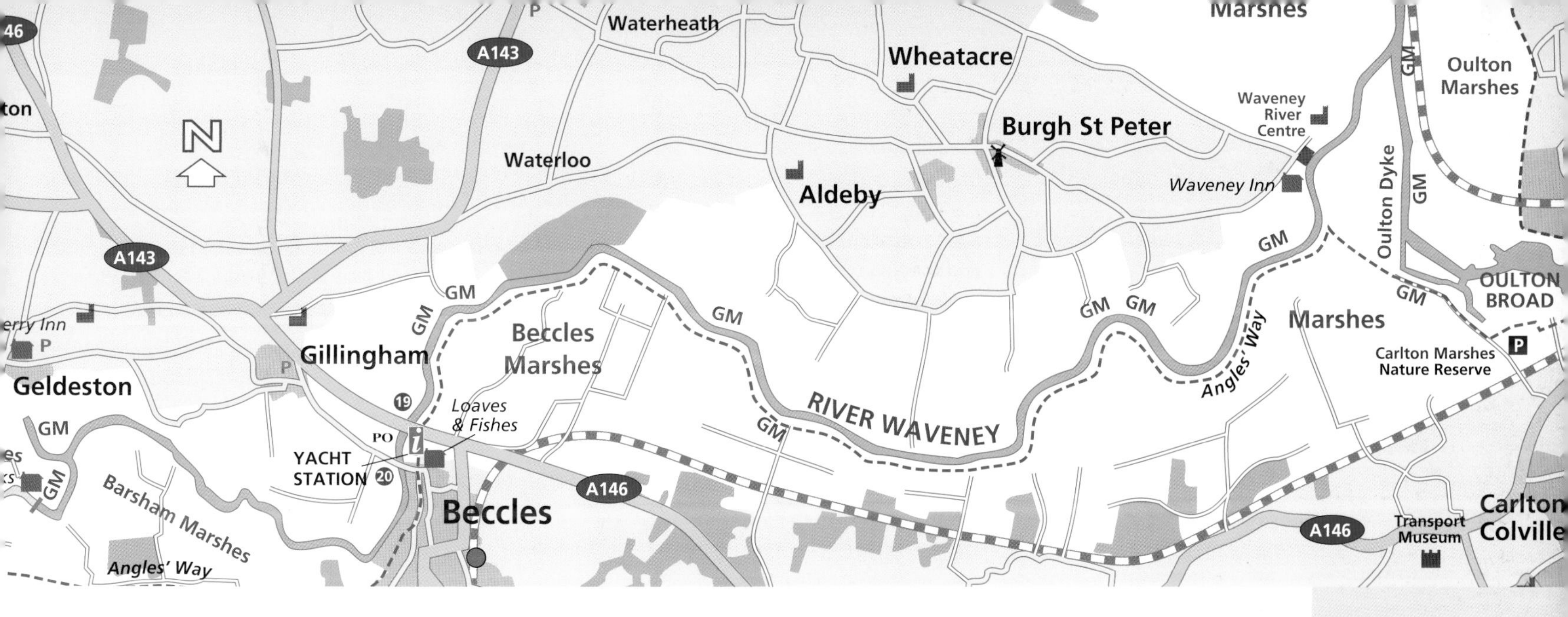

ʒeccles Yacht Station. Accessible toilets, vashing machine, tumble dryer. Tel: 01502 ʼ12225

:.C. Marine, Wherry Boat Yard. Dayboats, ›utboard and inboard repairs, breakdown ›ervice. Tel: 01502 713703

ɪ.E. Hipperson, Gillingham Dam. ɔruisers, electric dayboats, Caravan ɔlub CL site, electric points, storage. el: 01502 712166 PO WC

ɔcks Inn, Geldeston

Geldeston Lock

At Geldeston a dyke to the right leads to the village, where there is a pub, post office, phone and boatyard. The river to the left leads to the head of navigation at the lock and the Locks Inn. Moorings can be found on either side of the river. Fishing is good here. There is generally a good depth of water. The rise and fall of tide is from 61 to 76 cm *[2 ft–2 ft 6 in]*. At the lock the high and low tides are about 3½ hours later than at Great Yarmouth Yacht Station.

Pubs

Locks Inn, Locks Lane.
Tel: 01508 518414

The Wherry Inn, The Street.
Tel: 01508 518371

Boatyard

Rowan Craft, Wherry Dyke. Marina, slipways, canoes, Caravan Club CL site.
Tel: 01508 518205 PO

Bungay

This historic market town is beyond the head of navigation, but partly encircled by the River Waveney. It is 8 miles *[13 km]* from Beccles on the A143. The town has a Roman well, the remains of a Norman castle with a visitors' centre, a Benedictine priory and a buttercross. St Mary's Church is Saxon. There are a variety of local shops, including specialists in antiques, artefacts, curios and arts. The Waveney Valley Swimming Pool is on St John's Hill. Just outside the town, on the A143 at Earsham, is the *Otter Trust* (see page 25).

Website: www.bungay-suffolk.co.uk

Clove hitch

This is a useful knot for tying a light craft to a post or for temporary use, but can slip.

New Cut and River Yare Reedham to Hardley Cross

The New Cut

The New Cut

Dug in 1833 to improve communications between Lowestoft and Norwich, the New Cut is a canal 2½ miles *[4 km]* long, connecting the Yare with the Waveney just above St Olaves. The Haddiscoe Bridge, carrying the A143 near St Olaves, has at average high water a headroom of 7.32 m *[24 ft]*. There is a rise and fall of tide of between 76 and 91 cm *[2 ft 6 in–3 ft]*. High and low water are about 2½ hours later than at Great Yarmouth Yacht Station. There is no towpath and it is dangerous to moor in the New Cut.

Reedham staithe

Reedham

The New Cut joins the Yare just below Reedham. Once a Roman station on the large estuary, the village was built on high ground above the river. Traditionally it was the seat of Edmund, the martyr king of East Anglia. The church of St John the Baptist is a well known landmark.

Reedham is about 6 miles *[9.5 km]* south of Acle on the B1140. The rail station, ½ mile *[800 m]* from the river, has services to Norwich, Great Yarmouth and Lowestoft. There are two main streets - one on the higher ground and another beside the river. The lower street has a post office, telephone, provisions shop and takeaway food. *Pettitts Animal Adventure Park* (see page 25) and a small brewery are near the church.

Navigation and moorings

The rail bridge is swung open for river traffic when traffic permits. Craft too tall to pass under the bridge should sound a horn or hail the signalman, who should display a sign indicating the length of any wait. Cruisers can normally pass under the bridge unless there is a particularly high tide, but should watch out for larger craft if the bridge is open.

High and low water at Reedham are about 2½ hours later than at Great Yarmouth Yacht Station. The tide runs fast. The rise and fall is of between 76 cm and 91 cm *[2 ft 6 in–3 ft]*.

Moorings are free at the pubs, along the village quay and also at Sanderson's boatyard for short periods. Boats must be in a single line near the bridge. There is a Broads Authority quay attendant and rangers' mooring.

Boatyard

Sanderson Marine Craft, Riverside. Cruisers, minor repairs. Tel: 01493 700242 www.norfolkbroads.com

Pubs

The Lord Nelson, Riverside. Tel: 01493 701548

Railway Tavern, The Havaker. Tel: 01493 700340

The Ship, Riverside. Tel: 01493 700287

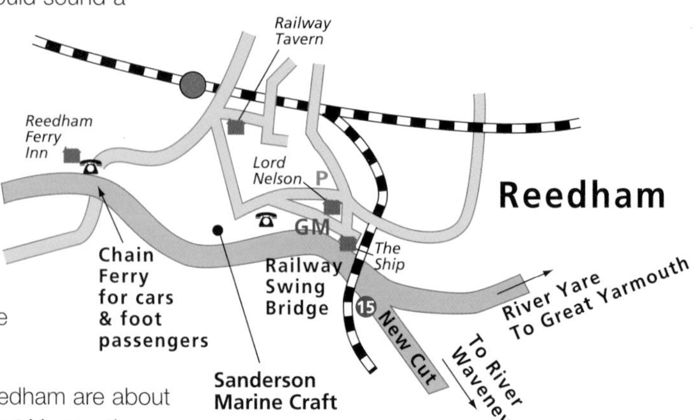

Reedham chain ferry

Reedham Ferry

Between Reedham and Chet Mouth is the only river crossing between Great Yarmouth and Thorpe – a chain ferry that should be approached with caution. There is also an inn and camping and touring caravan site on the northern bank. Moorings are free to patrons, with a phone, toilets and showers nearby. Reedham Ferry Folk Festival takes place here in late August each year.

The ferry runs every day of the week and can be in constant operation at busy times. The chain is hydraulically operated by a diesel engine and the boat accepts vehicles up to 12 tonnes in weight and 11.2 m in length. Fees are displayed on a board. The B1140 continues from the southern bank to meet the B1136, the route between Norwich and Great Yarmouth via Loddon and St Olaves.

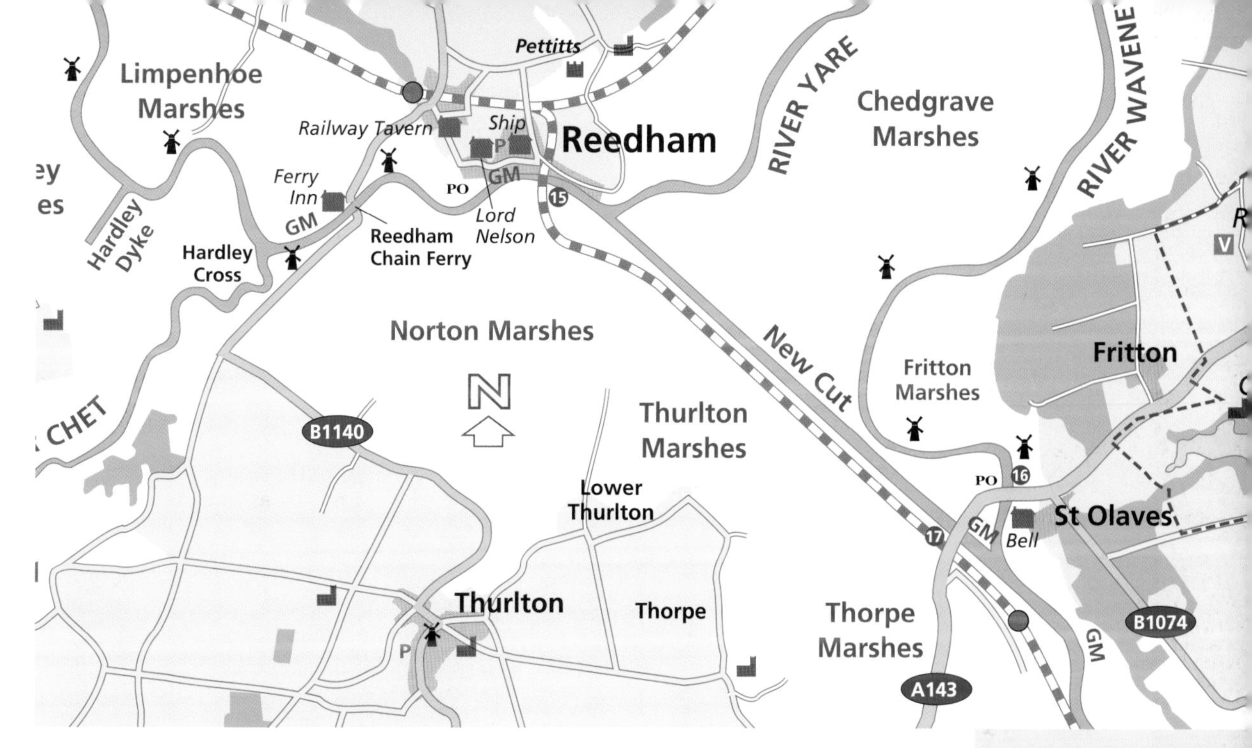

Reedham Ferry Inn

Pub

Ferry Inn, Ferry Road. Slipway.
Tel: 01493 700429
WC

Hardley Cross

One mile *[1.6 km]* above Reedham and 2½ miles *[4 km]* below Cantley is Hardley Cross, at the mouth of the River Chet. The cross marks the ancient boundary between the jurisdiction of Norwich and Great Yarmouth. The mayors of the two towns would meet here annually to judge the grievances of the boatmen.

Hardley Cross

Round turn and two half-hitches

This is the most secure knot for mooring. The end can be looped through to make a slipped half-hitch for quick release.

River Chet Chet Mouth to Loddon

Tidal flow at the mouth of the River Chet can be strong. The Chet is navigable for about 3½ miles *[5.6 km]* to the bridge marking the boundary between the market town of Loddon and the adjoining village of Chedgrave. The river winds through attractive wooded countryside and, although narrow in places, has a sufficient depth for all classes of hire craft, except at unusually low tides. About ¼ mile *[400 m]* from Loddon are the moorings for Pye's Mill picnic site. There are a few mooring spaces at Chedgrave Common on the opposite bank and footpaths to Hardley Flood nature reserve, where many types of birds can be observed.

All Saints Church, Chedgrave

Chedgrave

On the north side of the river, Chedgrave has a pub and a parade of shops, with provisions and a launderette, and a phone opposite. All Saints Church, which is Norman in origin, with a square thatched tower and arched stone doorways, is open every afternoon. Some of the ancient stained glass in the east window is said to have been brought by Lady Beauchamp Proctor from Rouen Cathedral. Beside the church, at the Pits, is a pleasant adventure play area for children.

Pub *White Horse*, Norwich Road. Tel: 01508 520250

Boatyards

Broadland Riverine Boatcraft, Loddon Boat Yard, Chedgrave. Cruisers, picnic boats, overnighters, canoes, cycle hire, private moorings. Tel: 01508 528735 www.riverine.co.uk

PO WC

Maffet Cruisers, Chedgrave. Cruisers, dayboats. Tel: 01508 520344 www.maffett-cruisers.co.uk

Pacific Cruisers, Chedgrave. Cruisers, dayboats, sailing dinghies, rowboats. Tel: 01508 520321 www.pacificcruisers.co.uk

PO WC

Loddon

Loddon is a pleasant small town with many Georgian redbrick houses, an unhurried atmosphere and a long-standing reputation for hospitality. There is a very wide range of shops and other facilities, including a supermarket, restaurants and takeaways.

The fine Holy Trinity Church, which stands at the heart of the town, dates from the end of the fifteenth century and has many interesting features. Typical of many

View from Loddon staithe

Norfolk churches, it is built of flint flushwork in the Perpendicular style. Above the porch is the Priest's Room, which holds a permanent exhibition of historical information about the area.

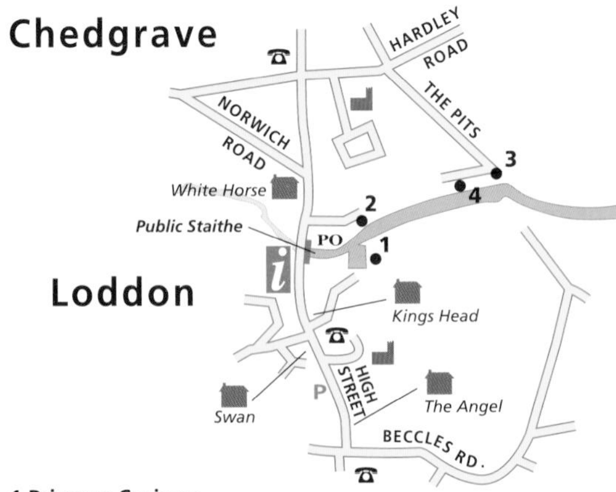

1 Princess Cruisers
2 Broadland Riverine Boatcraft
3 Maffett Cruisers
4 Pacific Cruisers

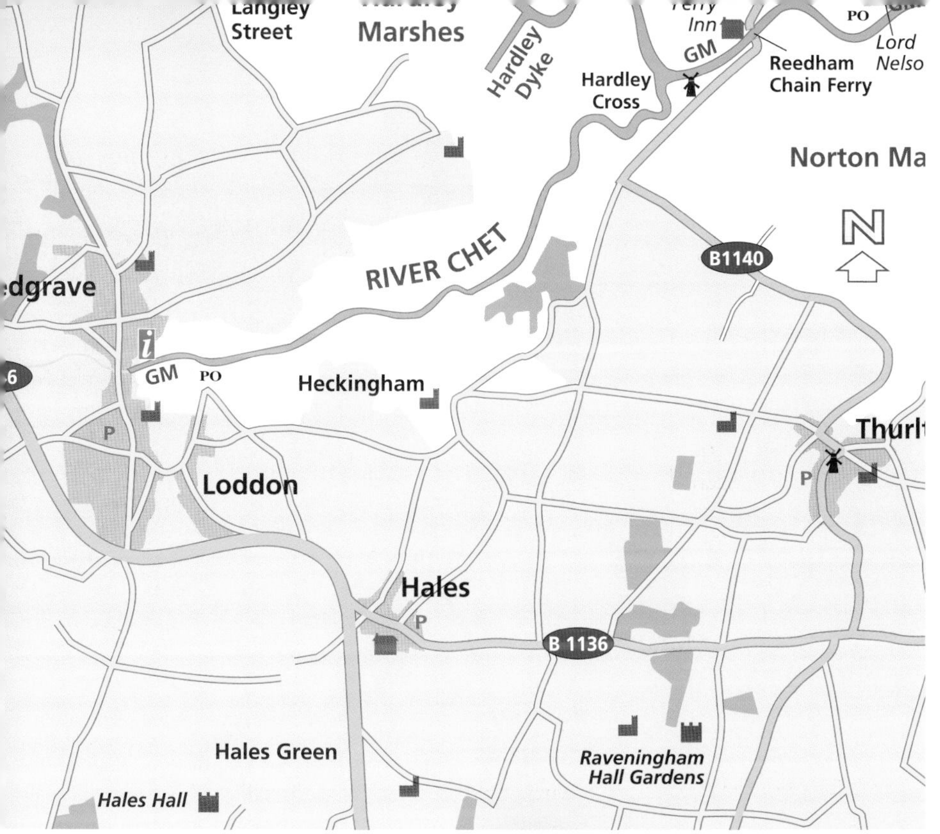

Nearby attractions include *Station 146 Control Tower* at Seething airfield, about 4 miles *[6.4 km]* W of Loddon off A146 (see page 29). *Hales Hall*, about 2 miles *[3.2 km]* S of Loddon off A146 at Hales Green, is the site of the largest brick medieval barn in Britain and home of East Anglia's first plant nursery, and *Raveningham Hall Gardens* are about 2 miles *[3.2 km]* E of Loddon, off A146 and B1136 (see page 27).

Website: www.loddon.org.uk

Holy Trinity Church, Loddon

Giant Hogweed – a cause of allergic reactions

Navigation and moorings

High and low water at Loddon are about three hours later than at Great Yarmouth Yacht Station. The rise and fall averages 76 cm *[2 ft 6 in]* and the tidal flow is moderate.

All the boatyards at Chedgrave and Loddon provide good moorings and there is stern-first mooring at the town staithe in attractive surroundings by the bridge, where there are toilets and water.

Boatyard

Princess Cruisers, Bridge Street. Cruisers, dayboats, dinghies, caravan site, private moorings. Tel: 01508 520353

PO WC

Pubs *The Angel*, High Street.
Tel: 01508 520763

Kings Head, Bridge Street.
Tel: 01508 520330

The Swan, Church Plain.
Tel: 01508 520239

Curlew

Numenius arquata arquata

The curlew has a haunting musical cry and a distinctive long curved bill. Its plumage is brown, with streaks and patterns, and it has a white belly and rump. It can be seen on mudflats and at the coast, and feeds on water creatures, worms, insects and berries.

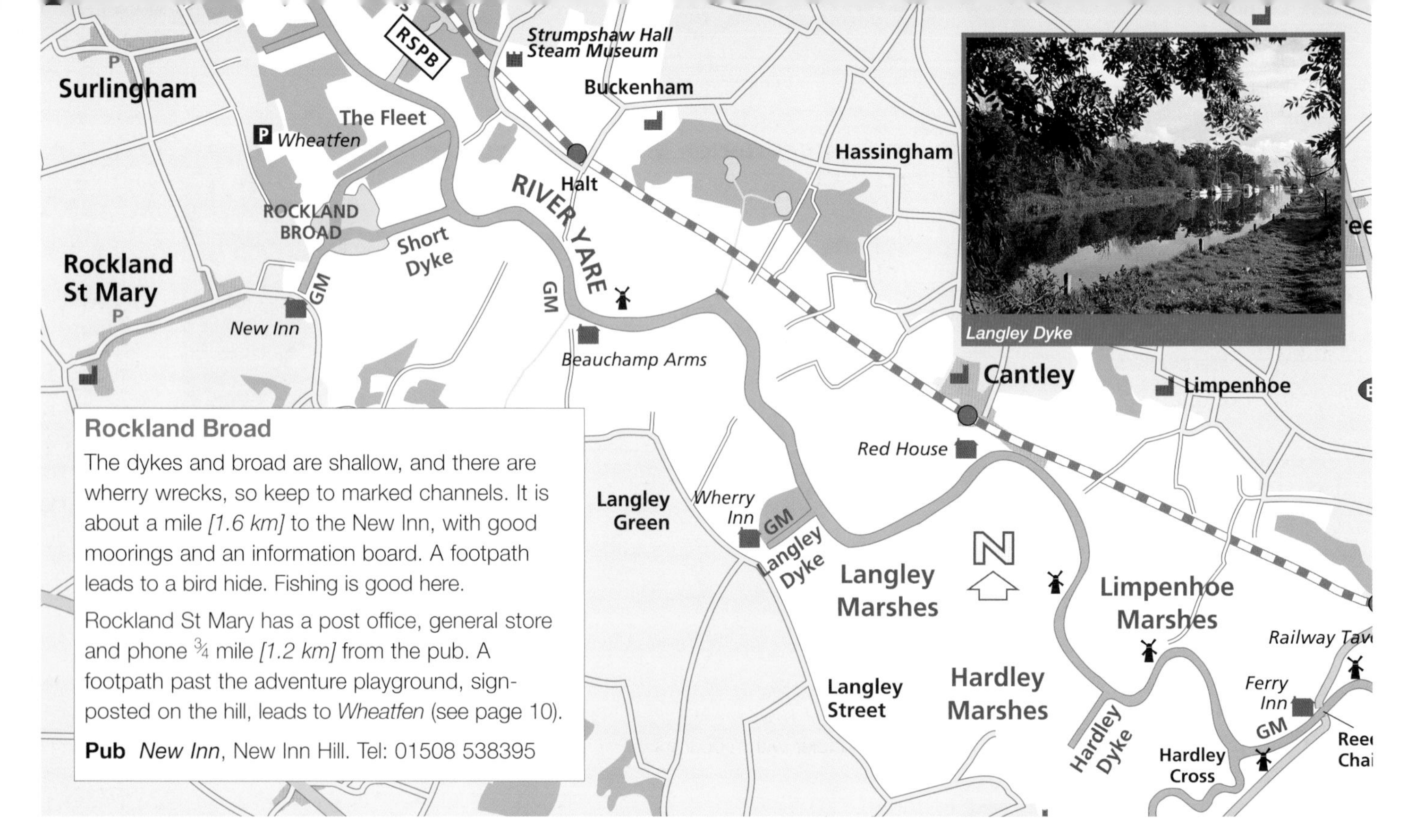

Langley Dyke

Rockland Broad

The dykes and broad are shallow, and there are wherry wrecks, so keep to marked channels. It is about a mile *[1.6 km]* to the New Inn, with good moorings and an information board. A footpath leads to a bird hide. Fishing is good here.

Rockland St Mary has a post office, general store and phone ¾ mile *[1.2 km]* from the pub. A footpath past the adventure playground, sign-posted on the hill, leads to *Wheatfen* (see page 10).

Pub *New Inn*, New Inn Hill. Tel: 01508 538395

River Yare

Chet Mouth to Rockland

Cantley

Moorings are few before the pub at Cantley, beyond the first sugarbeet factory to be built in this country, where coasters still occasionally deliver fuel. Cantley has rail services to Norwich, Great Yarmouth and Lowestoft.

High and low water are about 3¼ hours after Great Yarmouth Yacht Station. Rise and fall is about 84 cm *[2 ft 9 in]*. The next moorings are upriver at Cantley RSPB reserve.

Pub *Red House Inn*, Station Road. Tel: 01493 700801

Langley Dyke

Langley Dyke is 1 mile *[1.6 km]* above Cantley and 2 miles *[3.2 km]* below Buckenham. Nearby are fragmentary remains of Langley Abbey. There are moorings at the public staithe and at the quayheading along the river. The tide runs fast, so care is necessary. Safe moorings for small cruisers can be found in the dyke.

Pub *Wherry Inn*, Langley Street. Tel: 01508 528085

Buckenham Ferry

No ferry has served here since the Second World War. The Beauchamp Arms, on the south bank, has moorings and can be reached from the A146. Buckenham Sailing Club is based downstream of the pub. High and low water are about 3½ hours after Great Yarmouth Yacht Station. Rise and fall is from 61 to 76 cm *[2 ft–2 ft 6 in]*.

The rail halt is ½ mile *[800 m]* N, with Buckenham just beyond, 3 miles *[4.8 km]* S of the A47.

Pub *Beauchamp Arms*, Carleton St Peter. Tel: 01508 480247

?trumpshaw Fen, north of the river, is an ?SPB nature reserve (see page 10). Access ?y road is from the A47. *Strumpshaw Hall ?team Museum* is also nearby (see page 29).

?oldham Hall Tavern

?oldham Hall

?oldham Hall stands on a lovely part of ?e River Yare. Just upstream of Hobro's ?yke, it has an extensive quay and ?arden, and can be reached by road from ?e A146 through Surlingham. The ?oldham Hall Regatta takes place in May ?ach year. High and low water are about ?ur hours later than Great Yarmouth Yacht ?tation. Average rise and fall is 76 cm *? ft 6 in]*.

?ust above Coldham Hall is an entrance to ?urlingham Broad – a maze of waterways ? the care of the Norfolk Wildlife Trust.

?ub

?oldham Hall Tavern, Surlingham.
?el: 01508 538591

Surlingham Broad

Brundall

Hobro's Dyke, north of the river, is the site of most of the Brundall boatyards. On the river is an extensive holiday development where moorings, holiday chalets and houseboats can be rented. There is a general store and chandler with moorings further upstream.

A large village on high ground to the north of the river, Brundall has shops and other facilities, mainly on one long street. By road it is about 7 miles *[11 km]* to Norwich via the A47 and by water 8½ miles *[13.5 km]* to Norwich Yacht Station. The two railway stations have services to Norwich, Great Yarmouth and Lowestoft. There are also regular buses. St Laurence's Church has a thirteenth-century font, curiously covered with lead.

Navigation and moorings

High and low water are about four hours later than at Great Yarmouth Yacht Station. There is a rise and fall of about 61 cm *[2 ft]*. There is every facility for mooring at the boatyards.

Boatyards and cottages

Alexander Cruisers, Riverside. Cruisers.
Tel: 0870 2202498 www.blakes.co.uk
PO

Alpha Craft, Riverside. Cruisers.
Tel: 01603 713265
www.norfolkbroadsboatingholidays.com
PO

Bees Boats, Riverside. Cruisers, dayboats, fishing boats, launderette.
Tel: 01603 713446
PO

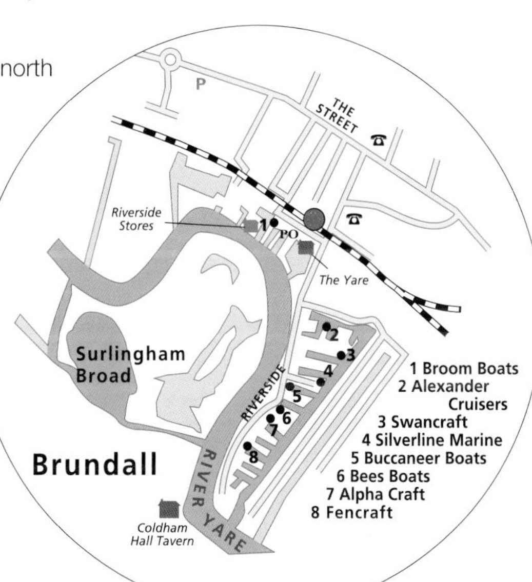

Marsh harrier

Circus aeruginosus

This rare bird of prey breeds in Norfolk and can be seen hovering over the reedbeds at Strumpshaw. The male is brown with light grey on part of the wing and tail, and black tips to its wings. The young male and the female are a richer brown, with a creamy tinge to the head and shoulders. Nests are hidden in the deepest reedbeds.

River Yare Rockland to Thorpe

Broom Boats, Riverside. Cruisers, chalets. Tel: 01603 712334 www.broomboats.com
PO WC

Buccaneer Boats, Riverside. Houseboats, dayboats. Tel: 01603 712057 **PO**

Fencraft, Riverside. Cruisers, dayboats, chalets, accessible toilet. Tel: 01603 715011 **PO WC**

Silverline Marine, Riverside. Cruisers. Tel: 01603 712247 **PO WC**

Swancraft, Riverside. Cruisers. Tel: 01603 712362 www.swancraft.co.uk
PO WC

Pubs *The Ram Inn*, The Street. Tel: 01603 716926
The Yare, Station Road. Tel: 01603 713786

Surlingham

Surlingham Ferry House is 1½ miles *[2.4 km]* above Brundall and 1¾ miles *[2.8 km]* from Bramerton Wood's End and has extensive moorings, but no ferry. High and low water are about 4¼ hours later than Great Yarmouth Yacht Station. Rise and fall is about 61 cm *[2 ft]*.

Surlingham village is 1 mile *[1.6 km]* south of the former ferry and has a post office and general store. A road and footpath lead down from the village pond to Coldham Hall.

St Mary's Church is of flint and stone in the Gothic style. Half a mile away, on a hill overlooking the Yare valley, stand the ruins of St Saviour's Church. *Wheatfen*, the nature reserve home of Ted Ellis, is nearby (see page 10).

There is a circular walk around *Surlingham Church Marsh*, an RSPB reserve (see page 10), from Surlingham church. This reed and sedge marsh is a breeding ground for many water birds and summer home to several species of warblers and waders.

Pub *Surlingham Ferry House*. Tel: 01508 538659

Bramerton Wood's End

Many people consider this to be the most beautiful spot on the Yare. Bramerton is 5 miles *[8 km]* from Norwich and can be reached from the A146. There are public moorings at Bramerton Common and a quay at the pub with a small shop. High and low water are about 4½ hours after Great Yarmouth Yacht Station, with a rise and fall of about 61 cm *[2 ft]*.

Bramerton village is one mile south *[1.6 km]*. St Peter's Church was rebuilt in 1462 in the Early English style.

Whitlingham Great Broad

Pub *Wood's End*. Tel: 01508 538899

Whitlingham

The Yare makes wide sweeping turns shortly before Thorpe and it is dangerous to moor anywhere on the main river. This stretch of water is the venue of local sailing and rowing regattas.

On the southern side are the two broads of *Whitlingham Country Park* (see page 27), which are used for a variety of water sports. The river bus from Norwich calls here. Access by road is along Whitlingham Lane from Trowse, past the dry ski slope. The park is crossed by paths and cycleways.

The Buck, Thorpe St Andrew

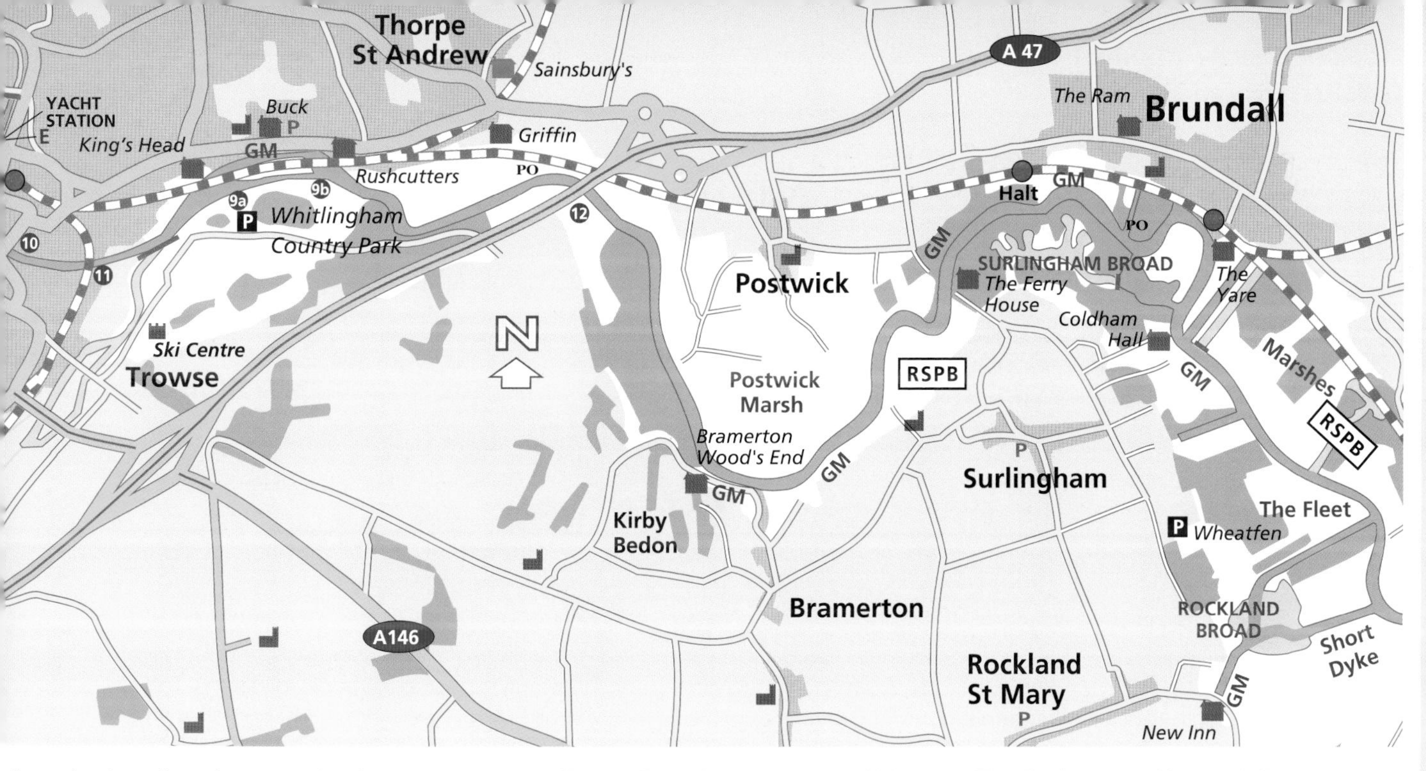

Eel

Anguilla anguilla

The European eel has a long snakelike body with no pelvic fins. Adults are metal-grey in colour with silver-white bellies. The dorsal and tail fins join to form a continuous edge to the tail end of the body. Eels are most active at night and sometimes travel short distances overland to pools.

ıformation boards at the car parks give ıore details about the area and wildlife.

ʌoorings

he dyke on the northern side has ıoorings and access to a supermarket on ound Lane, near the Griffin pub. High nd low tides are about 4½ hours after ireat Yarmouth Yacht Station, with a rise nd fall of between 61 and 91 cm *[2–3 ft]*. he Postwick Viaduct, which carries the 47 Norwich southern bypass, has eadroom of 10.67 m *[35 ft]* and stands at ıe entrance to Thorpe.

'horpe St Andrew

ust east of Norwich, Thorpe has pleasant ıoorings, both for long and short stays. uses and a river bus run to the city centre. Thorpe River Green is on the Old River. In 1844 the New Cut was dug beside the railway line so that river traffic need not pass under two railway bridges. This then became the main river. The River Green has a post office and general store, riverside pubs and St Andrew's Church. Headroom under the bridges at average high water is 1.83 m *[6 ft]*, but there are gauges to help navigators judge the clearance.

Pubs *The Buck*, Yarmouth Road. Tel: 01603 434682

The Griffin, Yarmouth Road. Tel: 01603 439211

The Rivergarden, Yarmouth Road. Tel: 01603 703900

The Rushcutters, Yarmouth Road. Tel: 01603 435403

Boatyards

City Boats, Griffin Lane. River bus, cruises, electric picnic boats, day cruisers. Tel: 01603 701701 www.cityboats.co.uk

PO WC

Griffin Marine, Griffin Lane. Fishing dinghies. Tel: 01603 433253 www.griffinmarine.org.uk

Kingfisher Cruisers, Bungalow Lane. Cruisers. Tel: 01603 437682

PO WC

River Wensum Norwich

A few hundred metres upstream from Thorpe, the main traffic enters the River Wensum, which joins the Yare on the right. The Yare to the left is not navigable by hire craft. Several bridges cross the Wensum in *Norwich* (see page 16): a swing bridge, a lifting bridge, a second swing bridge and others that are fixed. If the moving bridges are open, it may mean a vessel is coming through. The Carrow Road ground of Norwich City Football Club lies to the north just before Carrow Bridge. The round flint-faced towers on either side of the river are part of the ancient city wall.

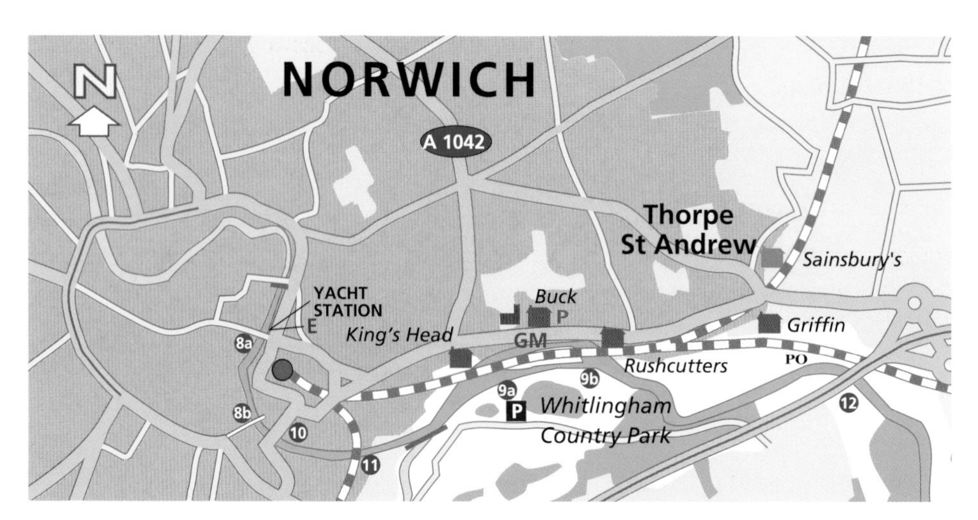

The old dock and warehouse area between Carrow Bridge and Foundry Bridge has been redeveloped with a swimming pool, bowling centre, multiplex cinema, night clubs and restaurants, a supermarket and other shopping outlets. King Street runs parallel to the left bank, with some of the oldest houses in the city, including *Dragon Hall* (see page 16). The Riverside Walk runs from Carrow Bridge through the ancient industrial heart of the city to Hellesdon, 5 miles *[8 km]* upstream.

River bus on the Wensum

The Novi Sad Friendship Bridge is named after a twin city. A second pedestrian bridge will cross the river close to Dragon Hall. On the right just below Foundry Bridge is the mainline Norwich Station. Local buses pass through the forecourt. The river bus also calls here, connecting with Wherry and Bittern Line trains.

Bishop Bridge and the Red Lion

Prince of Wales Road, which crosses Foundry Bridge, leads up to *Norwich Castle* and the city centre (see page 16).

The cathedral lies beyond the bridge on the city side of the river. Stone for the building was brought by river and up a canal through the archway of Pull's Ferry.

Norwich Yacht Station

Norwich Yacht Station is on the right beyond Foundry Bridge. Moorings stretch along the bank towards Bishop Bridge, the limit of navigation for hire craft. The head of navigation for all craft is beyond the city centre at New Mills.

High and low water at Norwich are about 4½ hours after Great Yarmouth Yacht Station. The rise and fall is between 46 and 61 cm *[1 ft 6 in–2 ft]* at the yacht station.

Norwich Yacht Station, Riverside Road.
Tel: 01603 622024

E 🚿 WC 💧

River Control, Carrow Bridge, Norwich.
Tel: 01692 678459

Jseful contacts

:mergencies

\mbulance, fire service, police
'ree service)

el: 999 or 112 Freetext: 18000

\ccident and Emergency Departments

Jorfolk and Norwich University Hospital,
:olney. Tel; 01603 286286
vww.nnuh.nhs.uk

ames Paget Hospital, Lowestoft Road,
;orleston. Tel: 01493 452452
vww.jpaget.co.uk

:oastguard Marine Rescue Coordination
:entre. Tel: 01493 851338

IHS Direct 24-hour nurse-led helpline.
el: 0845 4647 www.nhsdirect.nhs.uk

'orwich NHS Walk-in Centre, Dussindale
:entre, Pound Lane. No appointment
ecessary. Open Mon–Sat 07.00–22.00,
;un 09.00–22.00. Tel: 01603 300122

Pharmacists. Out of hours opening times are on notices in pharmacies and in local press.

Norfolk Constabulary. Tel: 0845 4564567
Minicom: 0845 3453458
www.norfolk.police.uk

Information

Broads Information Centres at Beccles, Hoveton, How Hill, Potter Heigham, Ranworth and Whitlingham (see page 8).

Tourist Information Centres

Aylsham, Bure Valley Railway Station, Norwich Road. Tel: 01263 733903

Cromer, The Bus Station, Prince of Wales Road. Tel: 0871 2003071

Great Yarmouth, Town Hall, Hall Quay. Open Mon–Fri. Tel: 01493 846345

Lowestoft, East Point Pavilion.
Tel: 01502 533600

Norwich, The Forum, Millennium Plain.
Tel: 01603 666071

ie River Yare at Surlingham

Websites

www.bbc.co.uk/norfolk
www.broadland.gov.uk
www.broads-authority.gov.uk
www.broads-society.org.uk
www.english-heritage.org.uk
www.english-nature.org.uk
www.edp24.co.uk
www.great-yarmouth.co.uk
www.great-yarmouth.gov.uk
www.itnorfolk.co.uk
www.lowestoftfairfestival.co.uk
www.nationaltrust.org.uk
www.norfolkbroads.com
www.norfolk-churches.co.uk
www.norfolkwindmills.co.uk
www.north-norfolk.gov.uk
www.norwich.gov.uk
www.rspb.org.uk
www.south-norfolk.gov.uk
www.suffolkcc.gov.uk
www.uea.ac.uk
www.uktouristinfo.com
www.visiteastofengland.com
www.visit-lowestoft.co.uk
www.visitnorfolk.co.uk
www.visitnorwich.co.uk
www.visit-suffolk.org.uk
www.visit-sunrisecoast.co.uk
www.wildlifetrusts.org

Roe deer

Capreolus capreolus

One of the two native deer species, the roe deer stands at between 61 and 76 cm *[2 ft–2 ft 6 in]* at the shoulder. The coat in summer is chestnut red to sandy yellow and there is a white spot on the upper lip at the side of the nose. Roe deer cast and re-grow their pair of three-point antlers in the winter. They browse on vegetation at all times of the day.

Index

Index

Text by **Bridget Lely**

Design by **Paul Westley**
Cover by **Kaarin Wall**

DTP management by **Martin Kempson**

Colour illustrations by **Paul Osborne**

Black and white illustrations by **Wayne Ford**

Acknowledgements
The author and publishers would like to thank the following for their help in compiling this book: the staff of the Broads Authority, local Tourist Information Centres and Great Yarmouth Yacht Station, and the many other local people who contributed their knowledge of the area.

Photographs by kind permission of the following: Broads Authority, front and back cover, pp. 1, 2, 3, 4 (bottom), 5, 6, 7, 8, 9, 10, 11, 12, 18 (left), 27 (right), 28, 29 (right), 30, 31, 33, 34, 35, 36, 37, 39, 40, 41, 42, 43, 44 (left and centre), 45, 47 (left and centre), 48, 50 (top), 51, 54, 56, 57 (top), 59, 60, 61, 62, 64 (bottom), 65 (right), 66, 67, 68 (left), 71, 72, 79 (right), 80 (left), 82 (right); Fritton Lake Countryworld, p. 70 (left); Peter Lely, pp. 68 (right), 70 (right), 74 (bottom), 75 (left and centre), 76 (left), 79 (left); New Pleasurewood Hills, p. 24; Somerleyton Hall, p. 26 (right); Thrigby Hall Wildlife Gardens, p. 25 (left). All other photographs by John Brooks at Pitkin Publishing Ltd.

Pitkin Publishing Ltd
Healey House, Dene Road, Andover
SP10 2AA

ISBN 978-0-7117-2999-5

Printed in Singapore. 2/08